AMAZING STORIES®

THE UNDERGROUND RAILROAD

Site of Lucy Maud Montgomery's
Cavendish Home

L. M. Montgomery

AMAZING STORIES®

THE UNDERGROUND RAILROAD

The long journey to freedom in Canada

L. D. Cross

HISTORY

James Lorimer & Company Ltd., Publishers
Toronto

James Lorimer & Company Ltd., Publishers acknowledge the support of the Ontario Arts Council. We acknowledge the financial support of the Government of Canada through the Canada Book Fund for our publishing activities. We acknowledge the support of the Canada Council for the Arts for our publishing program. We acknowledge the support of the Government of Ontario through the Ontario Media Development Corporation's Ontario Book Initiative.

Canada Council
for the Arts

Library and Archives Canada Cataloguing in Publication

Cross, L. D., 1949-
The Underground Railroad : the long journey to freedom in Canada / by L.D. Cross.

(Amazing stories)
Issued also in an electronic format.
ISBN 978-1-55277-581-3

1. Underground Railroad. 2. Underground Railroad—Canada. I. Title.
II. Series: Amazing stories (Toronto, Ont.)

E450.C85 2010   973.7'115   C2010-902657-8

James Lorimer & Company Ltd., Publishers
317 Adelaide Street West, Suite 1002
Toronto, ON, Canada
M5V 1P9
www.lorimer.ca

Printed and bound in Canada

FSC
Mixed Sources
Product group from well-managed
forests, controlled sources and
recycled wood or fiber
Cert no. SW-COC-001271
www.fsc.org
©1996 Forest Stewardship Council

Contents

Prologue

Was it safe? Susa slowly nudged the lid of the wooden box in which she had been hiding since noon. She poked a finger out, and through the narrow crack she strained her eyes to see in the evening dusk. Everything looked quiet but you could never be certain. Would someone come to get her or should she find a place to hide and hope to get some sleep? With a little luck, she would soon find a new life where she would be free to make her own choices.

It had been a long day. At dawn she had left the plantation where she had been born, she guessed, about seventeen years ago, and followed the wooden rail fences toward her destination. Hopefully, anybody who saw her would assume she was bringing water to the work crew in the upper field. She had thought about escape for many months but had not told anyone she was leaving. That way, nobody could be forced to say she intended to run away to freedom in the north.

But Susa was a house servant, not a field hand, and the rough ground had taken a toll on her feet. She sought the shelter of some scrub trees and followed them down to the stream. The water felt wonderful as she trudged on. The water was a good idea, she thought to herself, because the dogs would not be able to track her scent. That's how her friend Ben had been captured. The dogs had followed his trail up the road and across the pasture. He had been brought back in chains and beaten, but that had not lessened Susa's will to escape. She would just have to be more careful.

She had heard the whispers about people who were willing to help slaves get away. Some of the helpers were white. They hid you in their basement or gave you a ride under a pile of vegetables being taken to market. They gave you new clothes so you would look like all the other people in town. All you had to do was find the right people and you would be safe.

But how to do that? Her friend Matty had left last year and never returned. Before leaving she had whispered in Susa's ear about places up north where people did not have slaves. And she spoke, too, of a minister at the white church with a green door in the local village who would help get you started on your way to freedom. He and his wife would pass you on to somebody else who would bring you to a safe house where you could rest before starting the next part of the journey. How many weeks would all of this take? Susa had no idea. She just knew she had to try and, no matter how tired she became, she had to keep going. Staying a slave was not an option.

The stream passed under a bridge near the edge of the village and Susa climbed up to the side of the road, trying to clean her feet on the soft green grass along the way. The minister would not appreciate her dragging mud into his church. She had to make a good impression in order to gain his help. Looking off into the distance she could see a spire, so that must be the church. She could not see anybody, nor hear any traffic coming along the road, so Susa headed for the spire.

Luckily, the minister was outside sweeping the cracked wooden steps. From the tall fence at the side of the cemetery she could see him sweat as he laboured. Should she just walk up and introduce herself? What should she say? "Hello, I'm Susa and I want you to help me escape?" If someone saw them together they might call the sheriff and both of them would be arrested.

As she was trying to decide what to do, a horse and wagon pulled up and the driver shouted at the minister that he was ready to pick up the wooden boxes and take them to the store in the next county. The two men piled six crates onto the wagon and pulled up the tailgate. Then the driver walked down to the loading dock for a smoke. Susa crept forward along the fence and the minister spotted her. He held up his hand in a gesture that said "stop," then pretended to be patting the horse. Susa crouched down close to the fence and waited. She was so frightened she could hardly breathe and she could feel the front of her smock moving in rhythm with her pounding heartbeat.

The minister pointed to the fence and motioned for her

to run along it toward him. When she reached the wagon, he held up the lid of one of the boxes and said two words: "Get in."

Susa squeezed in, skinning her knees and banging her elbow on the rough wood. The lid slammed down on top of her. It was hot in the box. Not much air came in through the cracks around the lid, and it smelled of newly-cut wood.

She could hear the driver's steps on the gravel as he returned, then felt the wagon jolt as he climbed aboard. The horse pulled forward and Susa was tossed around inside the box. It was an endless trip. For the rest of the afternoon the wagon rattled along the bumpy road, stopping only for the driver to take a couple of breaks along the way. Eventually the wagon came to a halt at the back of a large building. The driver unhitched the horse and disappeared into the barn. Everything was quiet, for now. But Susa was hungry and thirsty and every joint in her body hurt. What should she do? She had to get out and walk, but in what direction and how far?

There was no turning back now. But if her luck held, she would soon be a person—not a piece of property. Susa gathered up all her courage and slowly, very slowly, pushed open the lid of the box.

Chapter 1
North America's First Blacks

Black Africans have been arriving in the Americas and in the region now known as Canada since the early voyages of discovery to the New World. Many were slaves—however, some were free.

One member of seventeenth-century explorer Samuel de Champlain's crew was African. His name was Mathieu Da Costa, and he is the first black African in North America who shows up in historical records.

Da Costa, or De Coste, a free black African, was a skilled linguist who spoke French, Dutch, Portuguese, and "pidgin Basque," a mixture of Basque and Aboriginal speech which served as the common trading language between Natives and the first Europeans during the early years of the east coast fishery. This dialect was understood by native North Americans such as the Mi'kmaq and Montagnais who lived on the north shore of the St. Lawrence River. Da Costa's linguistic skills were much in demand, and both the French and Dutch competed for the right to buy his services. This was not unusual. The tradition of using black interpreters was more than a century old at this time. When the French, Dutch, and Portuguese sailed down the west coast of Africa they often picked up—or kidnapped—African people who could help them communicate with the locals. Some they brought back to Europe to work in their homes and ships, while others they would display as exotic "curiosities" from foreign lands. These abuses then continued when Europeans and Africans sailed across the Atlantic to the Americas.

In February 1607, Mathieu Da Costa was in Holland. The Dutch had either kidnapped him or persuaded him to leave his employment with the French. The next year, Da Costa signed a contract in Amsterdam to sail to North America with Pierre Dugua de Monts as an interpreter. De Monts was the governor of Acadia, the French colony that had been established in 1604 in what is now Nova Scotia. Da Costa's contract was for three years with a salary of 60 crowns (195 livres), a substantial amount at the time. He accompanied de Monts and also Samuel de Champlain on one or more of their voyages to the St. Lawrence and along the coast of Atlantic Canada.

However, the well-travelled Da Costa must already have visited northeastern North America before the white Europeans for whom he was working. How else would he have already learned the language? He was able to conduct bartering sessions with the Natives, trading for food, fish, and furs and gathering information about the country further inland. He was also a deal-maker, incorporating Native gestures and grasping local customs to enable his employers to get the best bargain possible. However, there was always the potential for misunderstandings and violence, so it was also Da Costa's role to play the diplomat, charged with keeping relations between Natives and Europeans as calm—and lucrative—as possible.

But Da Costa, who was neither subservient to whites nor docile by nature, was not able to exercise diplomacy on his own behalf. In December 1609, he was imprisoned in Le Havre, France, for uttering "insolences" against authority. We do not know what he had said or whom he had insulted, but the French went to a lot of trouble and expense to retrieve him from the Dutch. There was a lengthy court case involving a merchant from Rouen who had acted for both the Dutch and de Monts and was seeking compensation. Da Costa was never heard from again, but his role in early Canada is commemorated with a plaque at the Port-Royal National Historic

Site in Annapolis Royal, Nova Scotia.

* * *

The first recorded slave purchased in the French colonies of North America was a child. In 1628, British adventurer David Kirke—who later became governor of Newfoundland—brought a young boy, about seven years old, from Madagascar to New France when his ships attacked and conquered Quebec. Kirke promptly sold the boy, who had been his servant at sea, to the head clerk of the colony, Olivier Le Tardiff. When Quebec was handed back to the French in 1632 by the Treaty of Saint-Germain-en-Laye, Le Tardiff, who had been friendly with the British, was forced to flee for his life. He returned to France. Not one to relinquish a valuable commodity, however, before he left he resold his slave to another Quebec resident.

Life then took a positive turn for the boy, who was educated by his new owner in a Jesuit school run by a priest named Father Le Jeune. He was also given a name. Taking "Olivier" from his first Quebec owner and "Le Jeune" from the priest, he was baptized in May 1633 as Olivier Le Jeune. He lived until 1654, but his death certificate shows that his status did not change during his life—although he was baptized, he remained an enslaved person.

Between Le Jeune's arrival in 1628 and the final British

conquest of Quebec in 1759, some 1100 slaves of African origin were brought to New France as household servants and farm workers. However, slavery in New France wasn't officially legalized until the *Code Noir* was passed by King Louis XIV in 1685. Until then, as elsewhere, the practice was tacitly condoned by the church and the civil administration.

The case of Marie-Joseph Angélique, a Portuguese-born black slave who was a house servant, is particularly tragic. Born around 1710, she became the property of François Poulin de Francheville of Montreal in the early 1730s. Being young and healthy, she was expected to have many children with male slaves as well as submit to the sexual demands of her master. But Angélique had other plans. She saw her future as a free woman building a life with her lover, Claude Thibault, a white indentured servant from France. Although she already had a son, born in January 1731, and twin boys born in May 1732 by another black slave, she planned to flee with Thibault to New England.

Her plans were foiled when de Francheville died suddenly and his widow told Angélique she was to be sold to the highest bidder. Angélique reacted to this news with fear and anger. On April 10, 1734, she set fire to her owner's house on Rue Saint-Paul, hoping the fire would distract the authorities long enough to cover her escape. The fire spread out of control through the wooden settlement and ultimately destroyed forty-six buildings, including Montreal's L'Hôtel Dieu hospital. However, the incident caused only property damage—no lives were lost. Angélique was soon captured and thrown into prison to await trial. Thibault managed to get away and was never heard from again. Following the rules of the French justice system, in a process that played out over two months, the chief investigator extracted her first "confession," in which she told the story of her life, and then a second "confession" by torture, in which she admitted her crime and was sentenced to make amends. She was to have her hand cut off (the one with which she set the fire) and then to be burned alive.

Angélique appealed, and the Conseil Supérieur modified her punishment but did not grant her a reprieve. On June 21, 1734, the day of her execution, she was driven through the streets on a garbage cart, a rope around her neck. She wore signs bearing the word *incendiaire* (arsonist) on her chest and back. At the front door of the parish church in Place d'Armes, she was forced to kneel and ask forgiveness from the King, God, and her fellow citizens. Her hand was not cut off, but she was thrown back on the cart, taken to the gallows facing the burned buildings, and publicly hanged by another slave named Mathieu Leveillé. The lifeless body of Marie-Joseph Angélique was flung onto a fire and her ashes were "cast to the four corners of the earth" as an example to any other disobedient slaves who were considering running away.

Angélique, like many black slaves in New France—which later became Upper and Lower Canada—worked as a domestic servant. Such slaves frequently served the same family for their entire lives but could be bought and sold and sent to another location at any time. About 60 percent of these slaves were male and 40 percent female. Some worked on the wharves and loading docks of port cities, others as rural labourers clearing land and tending crops. But unlike the plantation owners of the southern United States, who needed a great many slaves to work their fields, owners in Canada did not hold large numbers of slaves. That is why, when slavery was finally abolished in Canada in 1834, there was less opposition than in the plantation economies to the south where slave labour was essential to commerce.

A few settlers in Canada owned slaves, but usually no more than twenty. The Nova Scotia census of 1767 lists only 104 slaves in the province. But numbers increased dramatically when the United Empire Loyalists arrived, after the Americans had won their War of Independence against Britain in 1776. The Loyalists brought with them some 2000 black slaves: 1200 to the Maritimes (Nova Scotia, New Brunswick, and Prince Edward Island), 300 to Lower Canada (now Quebec), and 500 to Upper Canada (now Ontario).

Not all slave owners belonged to the white elite. The powerful Mohawk leader Joseph Brant (Thayendanegea) owned a number of slaves. In 1778 in Niagara he bought a seven-year-old black American slave named Sophia Burthen Pooley and her sister, who were daughters of slaves in New

York. Sophia was a domestic slave and remained in Brant's possession for five years: when she was twelve years old, he sold her to an Englishman named Samuel Hatt of Ancaster (Ontario) for $100. Sophia remained with Hatt for seven years. Correspondence shows that in 1801, Brant also considered buying a black slave named Peggy Pompadour who was owned by the governor of Upper Canada, Peter Russell. The sale apparently never took place, because in 1806 Russell placed a newspaper advertisement offering Pompadour for the purchase price of $150.

When she was interviewed in 1855—she was then in her nineties—for a book of fugitive slave narratives collected by Benjamin Drew, Sarah Pooley remembered hunting with Brant's children:

> *While I lived with old Brant we caught the
> deer. It was at Dundas at the outlet. We would
> let the hounds loose, and when we heard them
> bark we would run for the canoe—Peggy,
> and Mary, and Katy, Brant's daughters and I.
> Brant's sons, Joseph and Jacob, would wait on
> the shore to kill the deer when we fetched him
> in. I had a tomahawk, and would hit the deer
> on the head—then the squaws would take
> it by the horns and paddle ashore. The boys
> would bleed and skin the deer and take the*

*meat to the house. Sometimes white people in
the neighbourhood would come and say 'twas
their hounds, and they must have the meat.
But we would not give it up.*

Sarah also recalled how helpless she had felt as a slave
in the Brant household:

*I had no care to get my freedom [she had no
way to support herself]. Then I lived in what
is now Waterloo. I married Robert Pooley, a
black man. He ran away with a white woman:
he is dead. I am now unable to work, and am
entirely dependent on others for subsistence;
but I find plenty of people in the bush to help
me a good deal.*

The last surviving former slave in Upper Canada died
in Cornwall, Ontario, on January 17, 1871. John Baker was
believed to be 105 years old. He had lived through three name
changes of his adopted homeland—Upper Canada, Canada
West, and the Dominion of Canada. His mother, Dorine, had
been taken north when her owners, the Gray family, moved
from New York to Montreal after the War of Independence.
They then moved on to Gray's Creek near Cornwall. When
Colonel Gray died in 1796, Dorine and her children, including

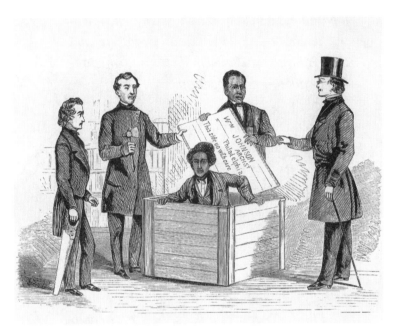

Some people hid in wooden boxes to escape.

John, became the property of his son, Robert Isaac Dey Gray, a lawyer who became Solicitor General of Upper Canada in 1797.

In a newspaper interview two years before his death, John Baker described his life, both as a slave and a free man:

> *I was born at Quebec, but brought up at Gray's Creek. My mother Dorine was from Guinea. My father was a Dutchman. He married*

*mother at Gray's Creek. Mr. Gray was colonel
of a Scotch regiment and wore kilts; was
married in the United States. I came to live
at Gray's Creek when a boy. Col. Gray's son,
Robert Isaac Dey Gray, was his only child, and
went to school in Quebec. He was a member
of Parliament for thirteen years running,
and became Solicitor-General. He studied
here with Mr. Jacob Farrand, to whom he was
related. The Colonel had much property. He
was strict and sharp, made us wear deerskin
shirts and deerskin jackets, and gave us many
a flogging. At these times he would pull off
my jacket, and the rawhide would fly around
my shoulders very fast. My brother Simon was
older than me, and was Solisary [Solicitor-
General] Gray's body servant. He dressed up
Simon better than himself. He took him to
Toronto with him. After Col. Gray died, Mrs.
Gray lived with the family of Judge Anderson,
who lived about two miles and a half west
of Cornwall. I lived three years in Toronto in
a large white house north of the landing. We
had in the house Solisary Gray, Simon, two
black women, and myself.*

The Underground Railroad

Through actions undertaken by the solicitous Robert
Isaac Dey Grey, the Baker family was eventually reunited with
John's grandmother, Lavine, also a slave, who had been living
in the United States. On a trip back to Albany, New York, in
1804, Solicitor General Gray wrote the following explanatory
letter to his cousin back in Canada:

> *I saw some of our old friends while in the
> States. None was I more happy to meet than
> Lavine, Dorine's mother. Just as I was leaving
> Albany I heard from our cousin, Mrs.
> Garret Staats, who is living in Albany, that Lavine
> was living in a tavern with a man of the name
> of Bramley. I immediately employed a friend
> of mine (Mr. Ramsay, of Albany) to negotiate
> with the man for the purchase of her. He did
> so, stating that I wished to buy her freedom,
> in consequence of which the man readily
> complied with my wishes, and although he
> declared she was worth to him £100.00, he
> gave her to me for $50.00. When I saw her she
> was overjoyed, and appeared as happy as any
> person could be at the idea of seeing her child
> Dorine and her children once more, with
> whom, if Dorine wishes it, she will willingly
> spend the remainder of her days. I could not*

avoid doing this act; the opportunity seemed
to have been thrown in my way by Providence,
and I could not resist. She is a good servant
yet, healthy and strong, and among you you
may find her useful. I have promised her
that she may work as much or as little as she
pleases, while she lives; but from the character
I have of her, idleness is not her pleasure.

Now that she was free, Lavine came to Canada and lived
for the remainder of her life in the house of Judge Anderson,
near Cornwall.

When his master, Grey, was killed in a boating accident,
John Baker, his siblings, and his mother were set free, as
directed in the will, and Dorine was given a small pension.
John went to live with a Judge Powell, then enlisted in the
army. He describes his service as follows:

First we went to New Brunswick; stayed
around that ugly, miserable place for three
years, till our time expired. Col. Drummond,
afterwards killed at Fort Erie, was our colonel,
and Col. Moodie, who was shot on Yonge
Street, was lieutenant-colonel. When our time
was out, Col. Moodie paraded our regiment,
made us a speech, and called on all who

wished to enlist to hold up their right hands.
All in the ten companies did so. We were after
this at Lundy's Lane, Fort Erie, and Sackett's
Harbor. We were at Waterloo, when Col. Hatch
commanded us; the 104th Regiment was
ours. I saw Napoleon. He was a chunky little
fellow; he rode hard and jumped ditches. After
that we came back to Canada, and got our
discharges in Montreal. I liked the service. If I
were young and supple I would not be out of
the army. The Queen now gives me a pension.

Some ten years before his death, friends of John Baker in Cornwall had arranged for a pension of one shilling a day for him from the British government. In his final years, John walked every day to the store owned by P. E. Adams on Pitt Street, where he did odd jobs. Between tasks he sat in a favourite corner of the store, resting his feet in the same place so often that the floor was worn down in that spot.

Chapter 2
The Railroad Starts to Roll

The Underground Railroad was not, of course, a physical structure. It was the name given to an undercover network of secret routes and safe houses that helped slaves from the southern United States escape to freedom in the northern states and Canada. It was operated by people—both black and white, on both sides of the border—who were opposed to slavery and wanted the practice abolished. These people were known as abolitionists.

The number of "passengers" on the Underground Railroad has been estimated as anywhere between 20,000 and 200,000, but the number most often quoted is around

30,000. Whatever the true figure, there is no doubt that this loosely-organized escape route was an effective conduit to a better life for many slaves. Along the way, ordinary people offered a meal, a place to stay, or safe passage to the next stop. Fleeing slaves were hidden in wagons beneath everything from sacks of flour to potatoes and pumpkins. Some were given disguises. Others were stowed away on canal boats, driven in carriages, or secreted inside railroad freight cars.

The term "Underground Railroad" arose from an incident in 1831 involving runaway Kentucky slave Tice Davids. To make his escape, Davids swam across the Ohio River, his master in watery pursuit by rowboat. A strong—and motivated—swimmer, Davids reached the Ohio shore near the town of Ripley just a few minutes ahead of his owner. Ripley was one of the earliest and busiest "stations" along the Underground Railroad. A light shone from Reverend John Rankin's house on a hill overlooking the river as a beacon to fugitive slaves. Fortunately for Davids, his owner lost sight of his quarry in the brush. Local sympathizers probably hid Davids in town and conducted him further along the route to freedom. In his frustration, the owner is purported to have said, "That slave must have gone off on an underground railroad."

The Underground Railroad in Ohio was efficient and well organized. Routes through forests, farms, and towns were established for safe passage from one hiding place to the next. Homes and barns with concealed rooms, secret hiding places, and hidden tunnels protected runaways until they reached the next safe haven. Almost 5,000 kilometres (3,000 miles) of routes crossed the state, most in a northeasterly direction.

The need for secrecy was essential, as the penalties for slaves or those caught assisting them were severe. Many slave owners chased fleeing slaves themselves or hired bounty hunters to catch them, and runaway slaves who had been returned to their owners were often brutally beaten. Ohio was a "free" state, but federal law allowed for the legal capture of escaped slaves from any free territory and imposed a fine of $500 on any person who hindered arrest or hid a fugitive slave. The United States Fugitive Slave Act of 1850 raised the penalty for assisting runaway slaves to $1,000, imposed prison terms, and required citizens to aid federal marshals to apprehend fugitive slaves.

Consequently, to maintain the secrecy of its operations, the Underground Railroad had its own code words:

- people helping slaves link to the Railroad were "agents" or "shepherds"
- guides along the way were "conductors"
- hiding/resting places were "stations" or "depots"
- abolitionist sympathizers arranged or fixed the "tracks"

- those who hid slaves in their homes were "station masters"
- escaped slaves were "passengers," "cargo," or "freight"
- slaves on the Railroad had a "ticket"
- financial supporters who funded the Railroad were "stockholders"
- the Big Dipper constellation, its bowl pointing to the North Star, was the "drinking gourd"
- the Railroad itself was the "freedom trail" or "gospel train"
- the Railroad led to "heaven" or "the promised land"— the northern free states or Canada

One of the Underground Railroad's most successful guides or "conductors" was Harriet Tubman. Harriet was born Araminta Ross—she later changed her first name to Harriet, after her mother—in 1820 in Maryland. Born into slavery, at the age of five or six she began to work as a house servant. Seven years later she was sent to work in the fields. While still in her early teens, Harriet suffered an injury that affected her for the rest of her life. Always ready to stand up for others, she had blocked a doorway to protect another field hand from an angry overseer. The overseer threw a two-pound weight at the field hand, but it fell short and struck Harriet on the head. She never fully recovered from the blow, which subjected her to spells of narcolepsy in which she would fall down unconscious. Her disability, however, did not stop her from helping many slaves escape bondage.

Around 1844, Harriet married a free black man named John Tubman and took his last name. In 1849, fearing that she and the other slaves on the plantation where she worked would be sold, Harriet decided to run away. She set out one night on foot and, with some assistance from a friendly white woman, she was on her way to freedom. She followed the North Star by night, making her way to Pennsylvania and soon after to Philadelphia, where she found work and started to save her money. She would need funds to carry out the rescue work she was planning.

The following year, Harriet returned to Maryland and escorted her sister and her sister's two children to freedom. She then made the dangerous trip back to the south yet again to rescue her brother and two other men. On her third trip, she went to rescue her husband. Harriet had used her wages to buy a suit for him before travelling south—but she reached Maryland only to discover he had taken another wife. John insisted he was happy with his new wife and wanted to stay where he was. Harriet decided not to make a scene, since he was not worth making a fuss over. Smothering her own emotions, she found other slaves who did want to escape and led them to Philadelphia.

By 1860, Harriet Tubman had made nineteen trips into the South and escorted more than 300 slaves to freedom. In

Harriet Tubman guided hundreds of blacks to freedom.

one account, when her passengers feared going any further, she forced the more timid ones to move forward by threatening to cut them with a sharpened clam shell, which she concealed in her clothing. Other accounts say that she carried a pistol. She told one escapee, "You'll be free or die." A few days later, the man was still with the group when they crossed into

Canada. She let it be known that "no foolishness would be indulged in on the road" and pointed out that "a live runaway could do great harm by going back, but a dead one could tell no secrets." As she once proudly pointed out, in all of her journeys she "never lost a single passenger."

During Harriet Tubman's many forays into the south, she devised clever techniques to help her and her passengers escape. She "borrowed" a master's horse and buggy for the first leg of one journey, leaving on a Saturday night, since runaway notices could not be placed in newspapers until Monday morning. Another trick she employed was to turn around and head south if she encountered possible slave catchers. And she carried a sedative to quiet a baby if its crying might put the fugitives in danger. On one occasion, she overheard some men reading her wanted poster, which stated that she was illiterate. She promptly pulled out a book and pretended she was reading it. The ploy was enough to fool the men, who let her pass.

By 1856, anyone capturing Harriet Tubman would have earned a sizable reward—wide-ranging sums from $12,000 to $40,000 have been mentioned, but no exact figure has been confirmed. Tubman was never captured nor were any of the fugitives she guided. Years later, she said, "I was conductor of the Underground Railroad for eight years, and I can say what most conductors can't say—I never ran my train off the track and I never lost a passenger."

Harriet's courage in the face of extreme danger was extraordinary. Of the famed heroine, who became known as "Moses," black abolitionist, suffragist, orator, and statesman Frederick Douglass said, "Excepting John Brown—of sacred memory—I know of no one who has willingly encountered more perils and hardships to serve our enslaved people than [Harriet Tubman]."

The John Brown to whom Douglass refers was another famous abolitionist, whose unsuccessful attack on the federal armoury at Harpers Ferry, Virginia in 1859 was one of the events that led to the Civil War. Brown was a friend of Harriet and conferred with "General Tubman" about his plans for the raid. He once described her as "one of the bravest persons on this continent." Brown had asked her to join him in his failed attack on the armoury, but on the night of the raid she fell ill. Her absence saved her life. John Brown was subsequently tried for treason, hung, then buried—along with two of his sons, Watson and Oliver, who had died in the raid—near what is now the Olympic Village of Lake Placid in upper New York State.

After befriending the leading abolitionists of the day, Harriet Tubman took part in anti-slavery meetings. On the way to one meeting in Boston in 1860, she stopped in Troy, New York to visit a relative and helped fugitive slave Charles Nalle who had been captured and was being held at the office of the U.S. Commissioner. Tubman gathered a large crowd and led them in an attempt to block Nalle's transfer by officers to a wagon that would take him back. The crowd surged between the wagon and the office door. Tubman cried, "Here he comes. Take him." She was hit over the head and punched but held onto Nalle. The crowd swept them both to the river bank where a boat ferried them across to the other side and out of reach of the officers. Nalle later bought his freedom from his master, who was his younger half-brother. During the Civil War, Tubman was a nurse, laundress, and spy for the Union Army.

One of Harriet's most challenging journeys was the one in which she rescued her seventy-year-old parents Benjamin Ross and Harriet Green who had eleven children, many of whom had been sold as slaves to owners further south. Tubman bought a train ticket for herself and travelled during daylight hours. This was a dangerous move considering the bounty on her head. When she neared their home, she bought a horse and a rickety buggy, bundled them on board, and drove her parents to a man she knew could arrange for their further passage to Canada. This "conductor," Thomas Garrett, helped her bring them north to St. Catharines, Ontario, where many of her friends and family had settled. Although both were free people at the time, her father was in danger of being arrested for hiding escaped slaves in his cabin—but with Garrett's help, they escaped.

After the Civil War was over, Tubman settled in Auburn,

New York, where she spent the rest of her long life. She died in 1913 at the age of eighty-one.

* * *

Like Harriet Tubman, Thomas Garrett also took enormous risks to help fleeing slaves. He was a great supporter of Harriet, who passed through his station many times. On several occasions, he gave her money and new shoes so she could conduct even more runaway slaves to safety. In 1807, Garrett, the eighteen-year-old son of a Pennsylvania land-owning family, had just returned home when his mother rushed to tell him that Nancy, a free black woman who worked for them, had been kidnapped by slave catchers. Garrett jumped back on his horse and galloped off, tracking them for 19 kilometres (12 miles).

When the slave catchers realized they had been discovered, and that they faced punishment for kidnapping a free black, they threw Nancy out of the wagon. Garrett pulled her up behind him on his horse and brought her back home. The incident made a deep impression on him, and he spent the rest of his life helping slaves and defying slave owners while running a successful hardware business in Wilmington, Delaware.

The authorities always suspected that Garrett was helping black slaves, but he was never arrested. He hid runaway slaves in his home or sent them secretly to other conductors on the Underground Railroad. If a new arrival was not being chased, Garrett would dress him in clothes like those worn by free blacks in town. He kept a wardrobe of costumes and a stash of old farm tools such as rakes and hoes hidden around his house.

At the crack of dawn, with rake or hoe over his shoulder, an escaping slave would walk purposefully up the street as if going to work for the day. Nobody paid any attention to him. Once out of town, he would hide the tool under a specific bridge just north of Wilmington and move on to the next "station." Later, Garrett would stop by the bridge, pick up his tools and bring them home, ready for the next passenger on the Railroad. When slave hunters came inquiring, there was no trace of the bedraggled escapee they described. When Garrett was directly accused he neither admitted nor denied his activities. The prosperous businessman simply refused to give any information at all.

On one occasion, the Garretts were amazed to see two carriages drawn by fine horses pull up in front of their house. They went out to greet their guests and found eleven black slaves who were fleeing from Maryland, 80 kilometres (50 miles) distant. In the first carriage was Harriet Shephard, the mother of five young children, who was determined that they would grow up free. She had persuaded five other blacks to come with them. They had "borrowed" the carriages and horses and set off at midnight. Late the next day they had reached Wilmington, asked directions to the Garrett house, and made their way there.

Garrett was not a man who usually acted swiftly, but on this occasion he had no choice. Two carriages, four horses, eleven slaves...the owners of all this property would be hot on their trail. The horses and carriages he held for return to their owners. The people, he believed, belonged to themselves, so they were taken to Pennsylvania where Quaker friends formed them into small groups and sent them north to Canada. The total number of escapees whom Garrett helped is not clear, but he claimed he "only helped 2,700" before the Civil War and the 13th Amendment put an end to slavery in the United States.

* * *

Another celebrated Railroad "conductor" was Laura Smith Haviland, a tiny white woman born in 1808 near Elizabethtown in eastern Ontario to American Quaker parents. When Laura was seven her family moved back to the United States, to a farm near Lockport, New York. Ten years later she married Charles Haviland, and in 1837 the couple founded a "manual labor school...for indigent children" known as the Raisin Institute. Haviland taught the girls household skills while Charles instructed the boys in agriculture. It was the first racially-integrated school in Michigan.

In the 1830s the Havilands started hiding runaway slaves at their farm, which became the first Underground Railroad station in Michigan. But in 1845 an epidemic killed Haviland's parents, husband, and youngest child, leaving her a widow to manage seven children, farm work, the Raisin Institute, and many debts. Still she remained involved in abolitionist work, and by 1851 she had moved to Windsor, Ontario, where she helped organize the Refugee Home Society—a settlement formed specifically for fugitive slaves and their families. There was a church and a school, and each family was allotted 25 acres of land to farm. Later on, the society would come to play an important role in the abolitionist movement.

Haviland also travelled frequently to the southern United States to help escaped slaves. Her first trip, in 1846, was undertaken to free the children of fugitive slaves Willis and Elsie Hamilton. Their children were still owned by their mother's former master, John P. Chester, a tavern-keeper in Tennessee. Chester had discovered where the Hamiltons were and sent slave catchers after them. When that failed, he had tried to lure them back by promising that they would be freed and reunited with their children.

Laura Smith Haviland was suspicious. She travelled to Tennessee in place of the Hamiltons along with her son, Daniel, and James Martin, a student from the Raisin Institute who posed as Willis Hamilton. Realizing he had been duped, Chester pulled a gun on them, threatening to shoot and to enslave Martin in place of Willis Hamilton. Laura's group managed to escape, but the Chester family would not let the matter drop. They hounded Laura Haviland for the next fifteen years. They challenged her in court, harassed her with slave catchers, and sent threatening letters.

One of these vitriolic letters reads:

> ...*By your cunning villainies you have deprived us of our just rights, of our own property...Thanks be to an all wise and provident God that, my father has...not [been] cheated to death out of their hard earnings by villainous and infernal abolitionists, whose philanthropy is interest, and whose only desire is to swindle the slave-holder out of his own property, and convert its labor to their own infernal aggrandizement...You can tell Elsie that since our return my father bought her eldest daughter; that she is now his property and the mother of a likely boy, that I call Daniel Haviland after your pretty son... What do you think your portion will be at the great Day of Judgment? I think it will be the inner temple of hell.*

Not a woman who was afraid to stand up for herself and her beliefs, Haviland responded with a dry wit, thanking Chester for naming the child in honour of her family and saying, "like Moses, may he become instrumental in leading his people away from a worse bondage than that of Egypt." It was then Chester's turn to extract a measure of revenge. He circulated printed fliers describing Haviland's appearance, her extensive abolitionist activities, and exact directions to where she lived. He finished off his hateful missive offering a $3,000 reward to anyone who would kidnap or kill her.

Haviland managed to evade all these legal and illegal manoeuvres while still visiting plantations. She pretended to be a white cook, and once a fair-skinned free black, all the time talking quietly to slaves, telling them about the Underground Railroad and helping them escape north. During the Civil War, she helped in refugee camps and hospitals near the frontlines, distributing supplies to displaced people, freed slaves, and soldiers.

After the Civil War, the Freedmen's Aid Commission acquired the former Raisin Institute, renamed it the Haviland Home, and converted it into an orphanage for black children. Its first residents were seventy-five homeless children brought by Haviland from Kansas. Laura Smith Haviland died on April 20, 1898 in Grand Rapids, Michigan and is buried next to her husband in the Raisin Valley Cemetery in Adrian, Michigan. At her funeral, hymns were sung by a choir of both black and white singers and her casket was carried by both black and white pallbearers.

* * *

Some slaves would seek out the Underground Railway or one of its conductors on their own initiative. One of these was Anna Maria Weems, a twelve-year-old house slave in Virginia who had been separated from her family and belonged to Charles Price, a slave trader who lived 24 kilometres (15 miles) outside of Washington, DC. After her mother and father had been sold to distant plantations in 1853, rather than remain a slave and be forced to bear children who would also be slaves, Anna planned her escape. She knew that owners often used young slave boys as carriage drivers, so she cut her hair short, dressed as a boy, and fled her Virginia master, hoping to reach an Underground Railroad safe house in Washington.

She made the first part of her trip with a posse of slave catchers in hot pursuit. A bounty for her capture and return was advertised in local newspapers. Anna Weems, like all fugitive slaves, was considered a felon, and helping a felon evade capture was a crime. Her case was considered dangerous and high-profile since she was "self-stolen"—having stolen her future labour from her owner, thus violating laws protecting private property. But luck was with her. When she arrived in Washington, she was able to find her way to a safe house.

Fugitive slaves often successfully used disguises, such as wigs, wide-brimmed bonnets, false beards, makeup, or cross-dressing, and Anna was no exception. Neatly attired, and giving herself the name Joe Wright, she again travelled undetected from Washington to Philadelphia. She stayed there for a few days at a safe house and was sent on, still dressed as a boy, to the home of businessman Lewis Tappan in New York. Tappan had been prepared to pay $300 dollars to bail out the man who had guided her on from Washington, and who had risked prison if caught. After arriving safely in New York, Anna found a home and friends with the family of Reverend A. N. Freeman.

Anna eventually reached the Buxton settlement in southern Ontario, where she was able to attend school. The Underground Railroad had successfully delivered another precious human cargo to safety.

Chapter 3
White Abolitionists and the Railroad

In 1793, the new province of Upper Canada (now Ontario) became the first territory in the British Empire to legislate against slavery, introducing the new law largely due to a single incident that had deeply shocked Canadians. In that year in Queenston, an enslaved black girl named Chloe Cooley was bound, thrown into a boat, and transported by William Vrooman, her owner, across the Niagara River to the United States, where she was to be resold to a new owner. She did not go quietly. William Grisley, a neighbour, heard her screams and witnessed her violent physical struggle against three male kidnappers. Under existing law, Vrooman was within his rights, as Cooley was considered a piece of property and could be bought, sold, or bequeathed to anyone he chose.

Grisley reported the incident to Peter Martin—a free black man and former soldier in Butler's Rangers, a British provincial regiment of Loyalists. The girl's plight was then brought to the attention of John Graves Simcoe, the first Lieutenant-Governor of Upper Canada. Martin told an executive committee, of which Simcoe was a member, that he knew of other slave owners who intended to do the same thing, thereby making a profit at the expense of someone's liberty. Simcoe was shocked. His reaction was to introduce a bill in the Legislature titled the Upper Canadian Act Against Slavery, which banned the importation of slaves into the new province. Simcoe was a staunch abolitionist who had been involved in the movement to free slaves in Britain, and the only person in the colony with the authority to introduce such legislation. The young Chloe Cooley's resistance had finally brought public attention to the issue.

Many members of Upper Canada's ruling elite, known informally as the "Family Compact," were already opposed to slavery on moral grounds, but those who still owned slaves resisted Simcoe's reforms. Hannah Jarvis, wife of provincial secretary William Jarvis, was incensed. She wrote: "[Simcoe], by a piece of chicanery has freed all the Negroes by which he has rendered himself unpopular along with White, the member for Kingston, who will never come in again [that is,

John Graves Simcoe, Lieutenant-Governor of Upper Canada.

be re-elected] as a representative."

Despite her bluster, she knew that no slave had actually been freed outright by Simcoe's legislation. The bill merely allowed for the gradual abolition of slavery. Political compromises had to be made to get the bill passed. So it was agreed that blacks could no longer be imported into Canada, slaves already there had to be properly clothed and fed, and children born of an enslaved woman would be free on their twenty-fifth birthday. But by the 1830s the Compact was losing its influence, and the Upper and Lower Canada Rebellions of 1837 and 1838 signalled the end of its influence altogether.

Although John Graves Simcoe's anti-slavery legislation was far-sighted—the first in the British Empire—it was not until 1833 that the Parliament of the United Kingdom passed the Slavery Emancipation Act, abolishing the institution of slavery throughout much of the Empire except for the territories in the possession of the East India Company, Ceylon, and the Island of Saint Helena. This finally brought an end to slavery throughout the Canadas when it went into effect on August 1, 1834. This gave hope to enslaved blacks in the United States who could reach that far destination. But they were hindered by the Fugitive Slave Act of 1850 in the United States, which placed all blacks and those helping them at risk of arrest and imprisonment if caught fleeing or helping others flee to Canada. Regardless, the Underground Railroad continued its work. Escapees who made it to Canada were the lucky ones.

A great number were helped by a well-to-do white opponent of slavery called Alexander Milton Ross. He was born in 1832 in what is now Belleville, Ontario, into a family that was firmly and actively against the practice of owning slaves. Ross attributed his "love of nature, and love of freedom" to his mother. When he was eleven years old, his father died, and Ross was forced to fend for himself. With confidence as big as his powerful physical frame, at age seventeen he travelled to New York City and became a typesetter at the *Evening Post,* working days at the newspaper while also studying medicine and remaining active in the abolitionist movement.

Ross graduated and became a doctor in 1855, but he was also a keen amateur ornithologist. He journeyed many times to southern plantations in the United States in the guise of a gentleman bird fancier, but along the way he was surreptitiously helping slaves escape to freedom in the north. During his travels, Ross held secret meetings with slaves, giving them information and supplies so they could find their way to Canada through the Underground Railroad. Sometimes he was able to provide a compass, knife, pistol, and food to aid their escape.

Ignoring the personal danger of being caught and jailed for helping slaves escape, Ross often accompanied small groups of black fugitives, escorting them under cover of darkness on remote routes to Niagara Falls and Windsor. But the greatest danger was to the escaping slaves. If captured, they risked beating, whipping, and mutilation. Many died as a result of such brutality, and family members who had been left

Dr. Alexander Milton Ross, ornithologist and activist.

behind were often punished for the actions of the runaways.

In later years, Ross wrote two memoirs describing his wanderings and his friendship with noted Americans like abolitionist and writer Ralph Waldo Emerson (who called Ross "my brave Canadian knight"), poet Henry Wadsworth

Longfellow, and President Abraham Lincoln, for whom he said he was a secret agent tasked with uncovering Confederate activities in Canada. He died in Detroit, Michigan in 1897 at the age of sixty-five, and was hailed as a crusader for individual freedom, especially for his work on behalf of black slaves.

* * *

Like Alexander Ross, John Fairfield also became involved in the anti-slavery movement at a young age. He was born into a slave-owning family in Virginia. When he was twenty, his uncle decided to sell a slave with whom Fairfield had grown up. Appalled, Fairfield helped the man escape to Ohio. His uncle was furious and sought out the sheriff to have his nephew arrested. When he learned what his uncle had done, Fairfield, who had inherited a great deal of money and had no financial worries, responded by taking a group of his family's slaves up through the hills of northern Virginia and onwards into Canada.

During the 1850s, Fairfield became an abolitionist and a clever conductor on the Underground Railroad, using obscure routes through Appalachia in a direct line to the border. He went to great lengths to create a false identity for himself in order to gain the trust of local authorities and move his passengers along. On one occasion, a group of freed slaves asked him to rescue their relatives who remained in slavery at the Kanawha River salt works. Pretending to be a businessman from Kentucky, and accompanied by two of the group acting as his slaves, Fairfield travelled to Charleston, where he befriended the slave owners at the salt works. He then pitched them a commercial plan to build boats to transport their valuable salt downriver, where it would be sold at a high price.

Fairfield was convincing. The slave owners fell for his ploy and he proceeded to supervise the building of two barges. Meanwhile, his two pretend slaves searched the surrounding area and rounded up their relatives, telling them to say nothing but to be ready to move quickly. When the barges were complete, they were quietly loaded—not with salt, but with slaves—and on a dark night they were sent drifting downriver.

Many hours later, Fairfield created an uproar, clanging dockside bells and yelling angrily to the townsfolk about the loss of his slaves and property. He gave an award-winning performance before organizing a search party to recover his "investments." He led the searchers around the region, but always further upriver than where he estimated his fugitive slave sailors would be. He suggested that the posse split up so they could search more territory, then meet back at a rendez-vous near town. They never saw him again. They never saw the escaped slaves again either. Fairfield had ridden in the opposite direction to the posse until he caught up with his fugitives and eventually guided them all the way to Canada. In other elaborate schemes, he pretended to be a slave trader, a slave owner, and an itinerant salesman. Adopting the persona of an undertaker, he managed to spirit twenty-eight slaves away in a mock funeral procession. Over the course of twelve years he made many trips into slave-holding states, freeing hundreds of slaves and conducting them north along the Underground Railroad. Then, just before the Civil War in 1860, he disappeared. There were reports that a man who looked like him died during a slave revolt in Tennessee in 1861. Apparently the man had recently arrived in the county and had been killed in a failed escape attempt. But nobody can say for sure what happened to John Fairfield.

Chapter 4
Canada Becomes the Promised Land

By the time a young Kentuckian slave named Thornton Blackburn came of age in 1830, self-serving pro-slavery ideology had transformed the institution described as "a necessary evil" by President Thomas Jefferson into a system slaveholders professed to be a "positive good."

Apologists for slavery maintained that white "wage slaves" working in factories in Britain and the northern United States were worse off than blacks living in slavery in the southern states. John C. Calhoun of South Carolina, who with New England's Daniel Webster and Kentucky's Henry Clay formed the "Great Triumvirate" of pre–Civil War

American politics, summed up this concept in a speech he made before the U.S. Senate on February 6, 1837: "Never before has the black race of Central Africa, from the dawn of history to the present day, attained a condition so civilized and so improved, not only physically, but morally and intellectually."

Nothing better contradicted such nonsense than the lengths to which enslaved blacks were willing to go to free themselves. The exodus of black men, women, and children from the slave states was a collective rejection of their circumstances and of the spurious rationalizations that supported slavery.

When the young Thornton Blackburn discovered that his bride, Lucie, was about to be "sold down the river" (the Ohio River) to the slave markets of New Orleans, he reacted with a daring and successful daylight escape from Louisville, Kentucky. It was July 3, 1831 when they made their break for freedom along the Underground Railroad. taking a steamboat up the Ohio River from Louisville to Cincinnati, and then a stagecoach ride to Detroit, Michigan. They integrated well into their new community, but two years later agents of their former owner were still tracking them down. The Blackburns were eventually recognized, handed over to the slave catchers, and imprisoned. The night before the Blackburns were scheduled to be returned to Kentucky in chains, Lucie was visited in jail by two free black women, "Mrs. Lightfoot" and

"Mrs. French." Mrs. French exchanged clothes with Lucie, allowing her to walk out undetected. She was then taken across the Detroit River to Amherstburg in Canada.

When Sheriff Wilson discovered that he had been duped, he threatened to make "Mrs. French" take the place of Lucie Blackburn and be returned as a slave to Kentucky. Although he was within his legal rights to do so, later that day he was convinced to let the woman go free.

Thornton Blackburn's escape was more difficult, however, as he had been shackled and was under heavy guard. But the next morning, as he was being escorted from the jail to the prison coach by his owner, the sheriff, and a deputy, the law officers were surrounded by a crowd of 400 blacks shouting and threatening them. Mr. Lightfoot stepped forward from the crowd and slipped a pistol to Blackburn, who pointed it at his wardens as he backed into the coach, locked the doors, and threatened to kill anyone who tried to recapture him.

Amidst the noise and confusion, the sheriff was fatally shot by an unknown protester. Blackburn was rescued from the coach and whisked away across the Detroit River to join his wife in Amherstburg. Meanwhile, the angry protest escalated into a two-day riot that damaged surrounding streets and buildings. When things finally calmed down, the rioters were fined and sentenced to community service, forced to repair the damage they had caused. Mr. Lightfoot was jailed for giving the pistol to Blackburn, and Mr. and Mrs. French fled to Canada.

The Blackburn Riots of 1833, Detroit's first racial uprising, allowed the Blackburns to escape, but they were still not safe. In June 1833, Michigan's territorial governor demanded the Blackburns' extradition from the British government in Upper Canada. The case was the first major legal dispute between Canada and the United States regarding fugitive slaves and the operation of the Underground Railroad. The United States petitioned for the Blackburns' return as criminals, but the Canadian court ruled that no accused person may be returned to a country where punishment is more severe than in Canada. This ruling is still in effect today. In Upper Canada (Ontario), Lieutenant-Governor Sir John Colborne refused to extradite Thornton and Lucie Blackburn, noting that a person cannot steal himself. The Blackburns were allowed to stay in Canada, which set a precedent for future fugitive slave claims.

The Blackburns settled in the new city of Toronto (formerly York) in 1834, where they became prominent and prosperous citizens. Shortly after arriving in the city they built a small one-storey frame house at 54 Eastern Avenue at the corner of Sackville Street, where they lived for more than fifty years.

He may have been illiterate, but Thornton Blackburn was smart and ambitious. He initially found work as a waiter at the Osgoode Hall dining room and saved his money, eventually starting his own business. When Thornton had been a slave in Louisville, Kentucky, transportation for hire was common, but he was surprised to find that Toronto had no such service. He decided to fix that. He obtained plans for a horse-drawn cab and contracted with mechanic Paul Bishop, who had a shop in the area, to build one for him. So Thornton formed Toronto's first taxi company with a one-horse carriage cab service, similar to those in Montreal and Quebec. He called his cab "The City" and painted it an eye-catching red and yellow. The carriage was entered from the rear and held four passengers—the driver sat on a box up front. It took passengers where they wanted to go for a set fee and was the start of public transportation in Toronto. In 1837, municipal records described him as "cabman, coloured."

For runaways like Thornton and Lucie Blackburn, the odds of making it to freedom were long indeed. Few chose to risk their own freedom and possessions to assist illiterate strangers, either black or white. But it was the outcome of the Blackburn case that confirmed Canada as the chosen destination, the final stop of the Underground Railroad. And the Blackburns reciprocated by spending their own resources to help other enslaved blacks settle in their new home. They never forgot the thousands of their fellow blacks who remained enslaved. Working with prominent abolitionists, Thornton and Lucie made their home a haven for runaways.

They became well-known and respected members of Toronto's African-Canadian community and helped build Little Trinity Anglican Church. Thornton participated in the "North American Convention of Coloured Freemen" at St. Lawrence Hall in September 1851 and was an associate of *The Globe* newspaper editor George Brown in anti-slavery activities such as lobbying government and associating with the Anti-Slavery Society of Canada.

However, the Blackburns never learned to read or write, never had any children, and no photographs of them are known to exist. In 1985, excavators in downtown Toronto did find the remains of a house, a shed, and a cellar beneath the old Sackville Street School playground. Municipal records listed the original owner as Thornton Blackburn. Dubbed the Thornton and Lucie Blackburn Site, it became the first archaeological dig of an Underground Railroad site in Canada.

Thornton Blackburn died on February 26, 1890 and was buried in the Toronto Necropolis Cemetery at 200 Winchester Street, on the west side of the Don Valley. He left Lucie an estate valued at $17,000, a fortune in those days. Many people remembered Thornton and wrote letters to the local papers about special trips they had taken on "The City." Lucie died soon after, on February 6, 1895, and now rests beside Thornton.

In 1999, the federal government Department of Canadian Heritage designated the Blackburns "Persons of

National Historic Significance" in recognition of their gener-osity to the less-fortunate, their lifelong opposition to slavery and racial oppression, and their important contribution to the growth of Toronto. In 2002, plaques in their honour were erected in Louisville, Kentucky, and in Toronto, Ontario. The Toronto plaque reads:

> *The Blackburns' determination to build free lives provides a window on the experience of many refugees in the Underground Railroad era. Having fled slavery in Kentucky, they were arrested in Detroit in 1833. Their capture sparked riots and in the confusion they managed to escape to Upper Canada. Here, the government twice defended them against extradition, and by 1834 the couple had settled in Toronto. Respected citizens, they established the city's first cab company, worked for Abolition and contributed to the well-being of their community.*

Chapter 5
The *Caroline* Incident and the Patriot War

Although Canada had become firmly established as the final destination of the Underground Railway by the early 1830s, largely as a result of the Blackburn case, many former slaves and their descendants were becoming unsettled by the political unrest brewing in their adopted country.

During the War of 1812, blacks in the Niagara area had been willing to prove their loyalty to Britain and fight any possible U.S. invasion that would threaten the small freedoms they enjoyed north of the border. Some joined the local militia, while others wanted to form their own company of black soldiers. At the instigation of Richard Pierpoint, a black veteran of the American Revolution, the government of Upper Canada responded by forming an all-black "Coloured Corps" of thirty men commanded by white officers. This "Corps of Men of Colour on the Niagara Frontier" fought at Queenston Heights and the siege of Fort George before being disbanded after peace was restored in 1814. In 1819, the government established the settlement of Oro for black veterans of that war.

But in 1837, the British colonies of Upper and Lower Canada (now Ontario and Quebec) faced a political crisis that was of serious concern to the country's black population. At issue was the structure of government and its control by a small group of aristocrats called the Family Compact. On one side of the political fence was a group known as the "Reformers," who called for sweeping political change. On the other side were the "Patriots," who supported the status quo. Eventually, the festering political dispute boiled over into an armed conflict that became known as the Rebellions of 1837, or the Patriot War.

In this war, Upper Canada's black population wanted to protect its rights as free men and women. They felt their best interests lay with the British, and they cast their lot with the pro-government patriots—who had long supported the anti-slavery cause—against the rebels.

In a letter to the American Anti-Slavery Society written long after the event, one of the rebellion's key figures, William

Lyon Mackenzie, stated what he believed to be the reason blacks had remained loyal to the government: "...I regret that an unfounded fear of a union with the United States on the part of the coloured population should have induced them to oppose reform and free institutions in this colony, whenever they have had the power to do so."

He was right. Blacks feared that any change in the political balance would negatively impact their already precarious situation. As a result, about 1,000 of Upper Canada's blacks volunteered to defend the government, and in 1837, a request was made to raise another regiment of black militia. In December of that year, a company of fifty black men was assembled in Niagara under white captains Thomas Runchey and James H. Sears.

The rebellion in Upper Canada began in the Toronto area and was led by William Lyon Mackenzie, a newspaper editor, merchant, and (much later) the first mayor of Toronto. He had constantly railed against rule by a self-selected elite and sought to correct the situation through armed revolt. On December 6, 1837, convinced that he would gain immediate public support, he led a ragtag group down Yonge Street toward Toronto with the intention of overthrowing the government. But Mackenzie had few skills as a military general, and his followers were dispersed by a few shots from patriotic Loyalist guards.

The following day, Mackenzie's poorly armed rebels

were again dispersed by Loyalists at Montgomery's Tavern near Toronto. Mackenzie then fled to Navy Island, in British territory above the Falls in the Niagara River. He still hoped to engineer an invasion of Upper Canada, with the help of some American friends. His approximately 200-strong Patriot force was supplied food, ammunition, and cannons by the American steamship *Caroline.* Sears's Coloured Corps was posted on the river opposite the island to keep the rebels pinned down, where they were once visited by Sir Francis Bond Head, then Lieutenant-Governor of Upper Canada. He later commented, "[Local blacks] hastened as volunteers in wagon loads to the Niagara frontier to beg from me permission, that in the intended attack upon Navy Island they might be permitted to…be foremost to defend the glorious institutions of Great Britain."

During the war, the commanders also used black volunteers to guard American prisoners, patrol canals, and protect bridges. They protected the Detroit and Niagara Rivers and the garrison at Fort Malden for five months, until May 1838. In all, five companies were authorized, although none were staffed to full strength.

On December 29, 1837, Allan MacNab, an influential member of the pro-government faction, ordered the capture of the little steamer *Caroline.* In the darkness of the night, a small British force crossed the Niagara River from Canada into New York State, boarded the ship, cut her loose, and set her on fire. Five men were killed in the attack and the flaming ship was set adrift downriver, where its remnants were eventually carried over Niagara Falls by the swift current. One crew member was killed and several were wounded in the skirmish.

Mackenzie managed to escape from Navy Island, but some of his followers were not so fortunate. Twenty were hanged for their participation in the rebellion. Twelve years later, Mackenzie, now living in New York, was pardoned and returned to Canada where he was elected to Parliament. William Lyon Mackenzie, leader of the Rebellions of 1837, died in 1861 and is buried under a large Celtic cross in Toronto's Necropolis Cemetery near the tomb of *Globe* publisher, opponent of slavery, and Father of Confederation George Brown, who had once run for Parliament against him. His tombstone simply says: "William Lyon Mackenzie, Born 12th March 1795, Died 28th August 1861."

The *Caroline* incident signalled the end of the Patriot War. But even though the rebellion had been quashed and their immediate concerns of annexation by the United States had been allayed, Canada's black population still faced a long journey in their struggle for recognition and equality.

Chapter 6
Spreading the Word

While the "conductors" and all the other brave people involved in the Underground Railroad network were guiding slaves to new lives in the north, others who were opposed to slavery were bringing attention to its evils. They condemned its practice in speeches, newspapers, and broadsheets.

One of those who helped spread the word was Henry Walton Bibb. Bibb was born into slavery in 1815, worked for masters in Kentucky and Louisiana, and undertook numerous breaks for freedom. He escaped to Cincinnati in 1837 and spent a few months in Canada in 1838, but when he returned to Kentucky in an attempt to free his first wife and their daughter he was caught and sold to a group of gamblers.

After another escape, Bibb finally made his way, alone,

to Detroit in December 1840, where he attended school for a short time. There, he joined the anti-slavery movement, travelling across Michigan, Ohio, and the northeastern United States lecturing about the wrongness of a slave-holding society. Bibb was an eloquent speaker, and his audiences were said to cheer and weep during his speeches. Two years after his second marriage—to Mary Elizabeth Miles, a member of the Boston Anti-Slavery Society—the Fugitive Slave Act of 1850 made it dangerous for the couple to stay in the United States. They crossed the Detroit River to safety and settled in Sandwich, Upper Canada (present-day Windsor, Ontario).

In 1848, Bibb published his autobiography—*Narrative of the Life and Adventures of Henry Bibb, An American Slave*—and in January 1851, he founded the first black newspaper in Upper Canada. *Voice of the Fugitive*, a biweekly paper, attacked racial bigotry and championed an immediate end to slavery, calling for the integration of black refugees into Canadian society. To the growing black communities of Detroit and Windsor, it also provided information about the Underground Railroad and warned against the threat of Canada's annexation by the United States, which at this time was still a slave-holding society. Bibb felt that the future for black refugees lay in becoming part of the greater community.

Bibb became a director of the Refugee Home Society organized by Laura Smith Haviland, an ambitious colonization project that proposed to settle some 25,000 to 35,000 fugitive slaves believed to be living in Canada. Supported by donations from American and Canadian anti-slavery groups, the Society purchased blocks of township land from the Canada Company near Windsor for resale to black refugees who had neither property nor funds to buy any.

Bibb would often greet newcomers personally and help them adjust to life in Canada. Each settler was given 25 acres on the understanding that five acres would be free if the land was cultivated within three years. The cost of the other twenty would be paid off in nine installments. The Society would use any profits to buy more land, build schools, and pay teachers. In January 1852, *Voice of the Fugitive* became its official mouthpiece until the printing office burned down in 1853. With help from the American Missionary Association (AMA), the society managed to settle 150 refugees before it was disbanded at the end of the Civil War.

The Bibbs initially thought they had found an ally in Mary Ann Camberton Shadd, a free black woman born in 1823, whose father's Delaware shoemaking store was part of the Underground Railroad. Mary Ann was a strong believer in integrated education, and even as a young woman she had echoed her father's view that education, thrift, and hard work were the way to racial equality and integration for blacks. Her dual themes were black independence and self-respect.

In 1847, Shadd published these opinions in a twelve-page pamphlet titled *Hints to the Colored People of the North*, in which she also highlighted the folly of blacks imitating the ostentatious materialism of whites. She urged blacks to take the initiative in anti-slavery reform and not wait for white support. In her lifetime she was an educator, abolitionist, author, publisher, journalist, and women's rights advocate, but she had two distinct disadvantages—she was black and she was a woman in an era when neither were treated equally with white males.

That did not stop her. Shadd became a leader and spokesperson for refugee slaves who had left the United States for British North America after the passage of the Fugitive Slave Act in 1850. In 1851, when Henry and Mary Bibb requested her help, she moved to Windsor in Canada where she started a new integrated school for local children. Shadd also provided shelter for numerous black refugees in her home, and in 1852 she published *A Plea for Emigration,* encouraging American blacks to immigrate to Canada.

But all did not run smoothly between the Bibbs and Mary Ann Shadd. Soon a conflict developed over the question of whether separate schools and communities should be created for blacks, or if they should be integrated with white schools and communities. The dispute was triggered when Mary Bibb opened a rival segregated school for blacks in 1853. Shadd openly opposed segregated communities like the Refugee Home Society, which the Bibbs had worked hard to make successful.

Soon after the society's incorporation, Shadd and her supporters criticized what they called its practice of "begging" for funds and clothing from philanthropic supporters. They charged that management was inept, and that management funds were being siphoned off for personal gain.

This dispute played out on the pages of the newspaper the Bibbs had founded, the *Voice of the Fugitive*. Bibb responded to Shadd's accusations in an editorial publicly questioning why Shadd had not made her school's grant from the American Missionary Association (AMA) known to her pupils' parents. The feud was damaging to everyone involved, and in January 1853 the AMA stated that it objected to Shadd's religious views and withdrew its funding. Shadd struggled to keep her teaching position from then on.

Shadd soon decided to start her own weekly paper in which she could control the editorial content. The *Provincial Freeman* began publishing in 1853. Accordingly, one of Canada's first female journalists also became the first black woman in North America to found a newspaper. But Shadd knew that a female name on the masthead would alienate many of the very readers she hoped to influence. Instead of taking that risk, she asked Samuel Ringgold Ward, black abolitionist and agent of the Anti-Slavery Society of Canada, to lend his name as the editor even though she was the driving force behind the scenes.

From the start, money was a problem and publication was intermittent. To raise funds, Shadd began a year-long lecture tour promoting subscriptions and interest in her anti-slavery, integrationist paper. It became a daily the next year. As a journalist and publisher, and as a teacher, writer, lecturer, and promoter of racial integration, she played a strong leadership role in Canada West (later Ontario). She always stressed that only integration could make blacks part of the mainstream and promote upward social mobility.

In 1854, Henry Bibb died suddenly at the age of thirty-nine. His wife, Mary, continued to teach, but in the 1870s she returned to the United States. In 2005, Parks Canada dedicated a plaque in a small park beside Mackenzie Hall in Windsor, Ontario, to honour the couple.

That same year (1854), Shadd had garnered enough support for the *Provincial Freeman* to resume regular publication in Toronto. With the motto "Self-Reliance is the True Road to Independence," the *Freeman* appeared on a regular basis again in 1857. Shadd used her newspaper as a platform to comment on black life in Canada, focusing on problems of racial discrimination and segregation. She targeted anyone, black or white, who might compromise on slavery, especially blacks who accepted second-class citizenship. She saved her harshest words for self-segregated black settlements, which she believed only promoted more discrimination, and she urged blacks to assimilate into Canadian society.

In January 1856, Shadd married black Toronto businessman Thomas Cary, and that spring returned to the *Provincial*

Mary Ann Shadd (Cary), teacher, journalist, and feminist.

Freeman after having travelled around the U.S. midwest on the anti-slavery lecture circuit. Shadd took a great risk as a speaker because she was a black woman, lived in Canada, and encouraged fugitive slaves to leave the U.S. As a married couple, they kept separate residences, she in

Chatham and he in Toronto. Their daughter, Sally, was cared for by her extended family. Shadd remained one of the three editors at the paper until 1859 when the financial burden became too much and publication ceased.

Shadd Cary, as she was now called, remained in Chatham and returned to teaching, all the while hoping that the Civil War in the U.S. would destroy the institution of slavery. She was part of a group that met with John Brown when he visited Canada, and she learned about his plans for a raid at Harpers Ferry in 1859. But she wanted to directly help the northern Union side against the southern Confederacy, and in 1863, after the death of her husband, she and her two children left Canada. She had accepted an offer by black field officer Martin Robinson Delany to be an enlistment recruiter in the United States.

After the war ended, Shadd Cary decided she could best serve her people by staying in the United States to help educate and integrate the millions of emancipated blacks. In 1868 she obtained an American teaching certificate, teaching briefly in Detroit before relocating to Washington, DC, where she received a law degree from Howard University in 1883. She was one of the first black women to do so. Her law practice focused on equal rights for American blacks. In her later years she was a vocal activist for women's rights, and she returned to Canada only briefly in 1881 for a suffragist rally. She died in 1893.

* * *

The voices of these black opponents of slavery were joined by a powerful white voice, that of George Brown, a Scot who had followed his family to New York, and then to Toronto. Brown was a reformer and later a Father of Confederation who founded the Anti-Slavery Society of Canada in 1841. He also published anti-slavery speeches, commentaries, and announcements in his newspaper *The Globe*, the forerunner of today's *Globe and Mail*. While the society brought together abolitionists—both black and white—from the church, business, the professions, and politics, *Globe* editorials opposed any real or imagined annexation overtures by the United States.

As a result, black Canadians enthusiastically supported Brown's political ambitions, hoping he would make changes for the better. He was not successful in gaining public office, but he was made a senator. Then, on March 25, 1880, an aggrieved former *Globe* employee, George Bennett, fired by a foreman for drunkenness, tried to shoot Brown at the newspaper's offices. Brown caught his attacker's hand and forced the gun down, but he was shot in the leg. What seemed to be a minor wound turned gangrenous and, seven weeks later, Brown died. He is buried at Toronto Necropolis Cemetery. Bennett was convicted of murder and hanged.

The Necropolis Cemetery (Necropolis is the Greek for "city of the dead") is the final resting place of two other notable black men who made their voices heard regarding the place of black people in Canadian society. Dr. Anderson Ruffin Abbott (1837–1913) was the first Canadian-born black graduate of the University of Toronto school of medicine, and he volunteered as a surgeon in the Union Army during the American Civil War.

Abbott's parents had been free blacks in Virginia who moved to Canada to escape prejudice. But as a black military doctor working in the United States he was only allowed to operate on black soldiers. When he returned to Canada he resumed private practice in Toronto and wrote articles about his belief that blacks should be assimilated into North American society, arguing that "it is just as natural for two races living together on the same soil to blend as it is for the waters of two river tributaries to mingle," and "the color line will eventually fade out in Canada." He died at the home of his son-in-law, Frederick Langdon Hubbard—the son of his old friend, black municipal reformer William Peyton Hubbard.

Hubbard (1842–1935), born in Toronto to former American slaves, became a popular city alderman (nick-named "the Cicero of Council" by his colleagues) who served as deputy mayor between 1906 and 1907—the first black man to hold both offices in Toronto. A baker by trade, Hubbard was recognized for his strong political opinions, his sharp wit, and his eloquence, contending that he had never experienced racism in political office because he ran on his knowledge rather than as a "Negro politician." He once asserted: "I have always felt that I am a representative of a race hitherto despised, but if given a fair opportunity would be able to command esteem."

Chapter 7
Josiah Henson and the Settlement at Dawn

Of all the blacks in Canada who spoke out against slavery, there is one who stood out as the leading spokesman for the country's growing black population. Josiah Henson was a black slave who eventually escaped to Canada, where he became a Methodist preacher, writer, and founder of the black settlement at Dawn near Dresden in Canada West (now Ontario). At his birth in 1789 in Charles County, Maryland he had been given the name of his first master, Dr. Josiah McPherson, and the surname of his master's uncle, "Henson."

When Henson was five years old, his first master died and the boy was sold to a man named Robb, who treated him badly. Robb later resold him to a man named Riley, where he was reunited with his mother.

As a young man, Henson was injured for life when his arm and both shoulder blades were broken by the white overseer of his master's neighbour. Despite his injuries, he became a trusted slave who was allowed to travel widely doing business in his master's name. But in 1825, Riley ran into financial trouble and transferred his slaves to his brother Amos in Kentucky. Henson was responsible for supervising the exchange and faithfully delivered all the slaves to their new owner's home. In so doing, he effectively rejected an opportunity to escape to Ohio.

At the age of eighteen, after hearing his first church sermon, Henson became a Christian and, during his three year stay in Kentucky, began speaking on religious subjects with the intention of becoming a Methodist preacher. In 1828, on the advice of a white Methodist minister, Henson used a trip to visit his master in Maryland as an opportunity to earn money by speaking as a lay preacher in various locations, hoping to raise enough funds to buy his freedom. By the next year Henson had saved $350, but his master reneged on the deal and demanded a new price of $1000. A disappointed Henson was transported to New Orleans to be sold once again. Luckily for Henson, his master's son, who was accompanying him, became ill and they had to return to Kentucky. This was finally enough for Henson. He would not pass up any more opportunities to escape. He fled, taking with him his wife Nancy and their four children. After a long journey through Indiana and Ohio, they made their way to Buffalo, New York, where, with help from the Underground Railroad, they crossed the Niagara River and finally reached Upper Canada on October 28, 1830. Like countless refugees before and after them, they were looking for a new life and the freedom to reach their dreams.

"When my feet first touched the Canadian shore, I threw myself on the ground, rolled in the sand, seized handfuls of it and kissed them," Henson wrote about his first taste of freedom. No more were they the property of another person. No more could they be beaten, forced to work from dawn to dusk for the profit of their owners, fed only on scraps of food, or housed under the stars or in windowless shacks. No more could husbands, wives, and children be split apart and be auctioned off like livestock. But it took tremendous courage to escape. Capture meant physical torture, and professional slave catchers tracked fugitives across the continent encouraged by large cash rewards from the slave owners. But thanks to agents along the Underground Railroad—men and women, black and white, Canadian and American— many slaves like Henson made it to the free northern states and Canada.

For about four years, Henson worked as a farm labour-er in the area around present-day Waterloo, Ontario. He preached occasionally, delivering his sermons from memory since he could not read or write at the time. He dreamed of establishing a totally black settlement, and finally, in 1843, he led about a dozen people to Colchester where they were able to lease some government land. Shortly after their arrival the group was elated to learn that, due to a clerical error, they would not have to pay any rent. Their short stopover turned into a seven-year sojourn.

While in Colchester, Henson met Hiram Wilson, a white missionary who had been sent north by the American Anti-Slavery Society in 1836 to minister to Canadian blacks. Funded by Wilson's friend, James Cannings Fuller—a Quaker philanthropist from Skaneateles, New York—Henson decided the settlement should be a registered black community exclusively for fugitive slaves, where they could live and choose how to earn their own living. With Wilson and a silent partner—probably Fuller—he purchased 200 acres in Dawn Township, Upper Canada, "for the alone [*sic*] purpose... of Education Mental Moral and Physical of the Coloured inhabitants of Canada not excluding white persons and Indians." He also purchased 200 acres of adjoining land for himself and his family, which they moved onto in 1842. The Canada Mission, a group originally composed of Wilson's friends in Ohio and later of philanthropists in upstate New

York, provided ongoing financial and emotional support.

The centrepiece of the Dawn Settlement throughout its existence as a living and working community was the British-American Institute, a school for all ages designed to provide a general education as well as teacher training. Established in 1842 as a manual labour training school, it provided functional instruction "upon a full and practical system of discipline, which aims to cultivate the entire being, and elicit the fairest and fullest possible development of the physical, intellectual and moral powers and to provide Black Canadians with the skills they need to prosper and to disprove the racist beliefs of proponents of slavery who argue that Blacks are incapable of independent living." Such stereotypes went as far back as Thomas Jefferson's 1853 "Notes on the State of Virginia" and persisted in newspaper articles and cartoons of the day.

Henson served on the Institute's executive committee until 1868. It not only directed the school but provided oversight of the community's farms, grist-mill, sawmill, brickyard, and roads. Settlers cleared their land, grew crops—mostly wheat, corn, and tobacco—and exported locally grown black walnut lumber to Britain and the United States. At its peak, about 500 people lived at the Dawn Settlement. Henson was recognized as the patriarch and preached at the local church but never assumed the official role of the administrative head of the community. This function was always filled by a white man: first Wilson from 1842 to 1847; then Samuel H. Davis of the American Baptist Free Mission Society from 1850 to 1852; and finally John Scoble, former secretary of the British and Foreign Anti-Slavery Society, from 1852 to 1868.

Henson, however, was always the community elder, the father of Dawn, and the accepted spokesman for Canada's black population. In these capacities, he raised funds by touring and speaking in the American Midwest, New England, and New York State between 1843 and 1847. As an active Methodist preacher, Henson spoke about abolition and slavery and told his own life story along Underground Railroad routes between Tennessee and Ontario. He was also invited to England for two speaking engagements between 1849

Josiah Henson on the first commemorative Canadian postage stamp to feature a Black Canadian.

and 1851, where he met both the Archbishop of Canterbury and British Prime Minister John Russell. On his second visit, between 1851 and 1852, he attended the World's Fair and became the first former slave to have a personal audience with Queen Victoria. She gave him a gift of her photo in a gold frame.

It was Henson's role as the settlement's spiritual and symbolic leader that brought him into conflict with the official administrators, causing the dissension that would eventually tear apart the Dawn community as well as other black settlements nearby. In 1845, the executive committee, Henson included, was charged by the newly appointed secretary with failing to properly administer the community's funds. Although a black convention at Drummondville (now part of Niagara Falls, Ontario) cleared Henson of any wrongdoing two years later, the trustees of the Institute condemned the entire executive committee as unfit to direct the affairs of the school. Further investigations in Britain in 1849 and 1852 also cast doubt on Henson's ability to manage the interests of the settlement.

These dissensions forced the resignation of Wilson in 1847, caused a failure of committee rule from 1847 to 1850, and shortened Davis's tenure. Even Scoble, who remained at Dawn for sixteen years, argued constantly with Henson over property sales, eventually resulting in several lawsuits. Scoble emerged victorious, and the Institute was closed in

1868. Later, after Scoble had left Dawn, the school assets were used to establish the Wilberforce Educational Institute in nearby Chatham. Dawn slowly disintegrated as funds dried up and its people drifted off to other communities in Ontario or returned to the United States, where slavery had been abolished after the Civil War. Although Henson stayed on in Dresden until his death, he was no longer the esteemed black leader of former years.

In 1849, Henson told his life story to Samuel A. Eliot, and the book was published as *The Life of Josiah Henson, Formerly a Slave, Now an Inhabitant of Canada*. The autobiography was reissued in many editions, with modifications and additions appended even during Henson's lifetime. Three years after the first edition was published, Harriet Beecher Stowe's book *Uncle Tom's Cabin; or, Life Among the Lowly* was published in the United States. Stowe acknowledged that she had met Henson and had read his book, so in the public mind Henson was her model for the fictional Uncle Tom. Henson did not discourage the connection and undertook lecture tours promoting himself as the "real life Uncle Tom."

Following the success of Stowe's novel, Henson issued an expanded version of his life story in 1858 titled *Truth Stranger Than Fiction. Father Henson's Story of His Own Life*, which was published Boston. In 1876, his finances now drained by his long court battles with Scoble, he returned to England to raise funds. He also made a brief visit to his old slave home in Maryland between 1877 and 1878, but then spent his last years quietly until his death at age ninety-four in 1883 at Dresden, Ontario.

Although Josiah Henson had taken part in abolitionist activity in the United States as well, his importance in Canadian history lies in his work at Dawn. It was here that he contributed most significantly to Canada's role in the North American anti-slavery crusade. Throughout his life, Henson was an important leader of Canada's growing black community. He had led a black militia unit during the Upper Canada Rebellion of 1837, was a strong advocate in support of literacy and education for blacks, and even helped black Canadians join the Union Army to fight against slavery during the American Civil War.

In 1983, Henson became the first black person to be featured on a Canadian stamp, when Canada Post issued a commemorative stamp honouring his life as a community leader and a conductor on the Underground Railroad.

Chapter 8
Black Settlers in Central Canada

The Dawn Settlement near Dresden was not the only choice for black refugees from the United States who had fled north, either on their own or with help from the Underground Railroad. Black refugees arrived in Canada at points as far east as Nova Scotia and as far west as British Columbia, but the vast majority landed in what is now southern Ontario.

Many Underground Railroad terminals were located in Essex and Kent counties and at ports along the Great Lakes; blacks from Cincinnati formed the community of Wilberforce near Lucan, north of London; and black veterans of the War of 1812 had been given land in Oro Township. It was only natural, then, that new black settlements would develop in these areas, where farming and forestry were the main occupations. Former slaves often chose to settle in areas that already had a high concentration of blacks for protection from the perceived threat of slave catchers, protection from racial discrimination, and for general community support.

By 1840, the black presence in Upper Canada extended in a triangle from Niagara Falls to Windsor and Collingwood. Of more than 20,000 who immigrated to this region, only some 4,000 returned to the United States after the Civil War. The 1861 Upper Canada census recorded "people of colour" in 312 townships and city wards, making them one of the most widely dispersed ethnic groups in the province at that time.

The Underground Railroad passengers were a diverse group. A few had money, education, and marketable skills, but most arrived with little more than the clothes on their backs. Those who could sought work on farms and, in time, bought their own land or moved to larger centres like the city of Toronto, where opportunities were better. The 1861 census listed more than 1,000 blacks in the city, most of whom had arrived by the Underground Railroad.

One of these passengers was Richard Pierpoint, whose journey began in Africa in the state of Bundu (also Bondu), now part of eastern Senegal, where in 1760 he was taken pris-oner, sold as a slave, and transported in the wretched hold of a slave ship to the British North American Colonies, where he became the personal servant of a British officer.

During the American Revolutionary War, Pierpoint enlisted on the side of the British army on the promise of gaining his freedom after the war. He was one of the few blacks in the Loyalist troop known as Butler's Rangers. After the war he was granted 200 acres of land on Twelve Mile Creek (now Grantham Township), which he later sold.

Pierpoint, also known as Captain Dick or Black Dick, was one of nineteen people who petitioned Lieutenant-Governor John Graves Simcoe in 1794 to "Free Negroes." They described themselves as veterans of the "late War... others who were born free with a few who have come into Canada since the peace...desirous of settling adjacent to each other in order that they may be enabled to give assistance (in work) to those amongst them who may most want it." They wanted Simcoe "to allow them a Tract of Country to settle on, separate from the white settlers."

Their petition was denied, and thereafter Pierpoint settled into life as a labourer. When the War of 1812 broke out, however, he seized another opportunity and proposed raising "a Corps of Men of Colour on the Niagara Frontier." Again his proposal was denied, but a small contingent was raised under white officer Robert Runchey. Pierpoint volunteered as a private and served from 1812 to 1815 before returning to live as a labourer in the Grantham area.

In 1821, Pierpoint was living near present-day Niagara-on-the-Lake when he petitioned the Lieutenant-Governor, Sir Peregrine Maitland, for help on the grounds that it was "difficult to obtain a livelihood by his labor," and because he was "desirous to return to his native country" in West Africa. Yet again his petition was denied, but he was granted a voucher for 100 acres of land along the Grand River near today's town of Fergus.

Two other members of the "Coloured Corps," Robert Jupiter and John Vanpatten, also received these grants for ex-military personnel. Of the three, only Pierpoint met his settlement obligations by clearing and fencing five acres and building a house. It was quite an accomplishment, as he was by then an old man.

In 1828, the lone black in a settlement of whites, he made out his will. Having no heirs or relations he left his farm and an unproven claim to a former lot in Grantham to a resident of Halton County, Lemuel Brown. Richard Pierpoint died in 1837, having never fulfilled his wish of returning to his home country. Pierpoint was unusual in settling in the midst of a white community. Most blacks in Canada, as mentioned earlier, preferred to settle within their own communities.

* * *

The heart and soul of these black communities was inavariably the church. In 1848, the growing Underground Railroad refugee community at Amherstburg, Ontario, began to erect the stone walls of a small chapel. These immigrants wanted to govern their own church in their new homeland, and they established a new denomination. They were assisted by Bishop Willis Nazery, who led many black Methodist Episcopal congregations into the new Canadian-based British Methodist Episcopal Church.

A large black refugee population also developed in the town of St. Catharines, due to its closeness to the border with the United States. In 1855, the congregation of Salem Chapel, B.M.E. Church often included newly arrived escapees who had been led to freedom by Underground Railroad conductor Harriet Tubman. Her "passengers" found shelter in a house where Tubman lived during the 1850s, just behind the church. Owing to her growing fame, the church became a frequent stopping point for many abolitionists from around the world.

The established church was also involved in enabling black refugees to settle in Canada. In 1849, fifteen former slaves arrived on the north shores of Lake Erie in Upper Canada, where Irish Presbyterian minister William King had purchased a 3,642 hectare (9,000 acre) plot of land for a refugee settlement. Here, newly arrived blacks would be able to purchase 20 hectare (50 acre) plots at moderate rates.

As a young man, King had moved to the United States,

married the daughter of a Louisiana slave owner, and became a slave owner himself. But by 1843 he had become disillusioned with southern life and slavery, and he travelled to Scotland to study divinity. Three years later, his wife and their child now dead, King was dispatched as a missionary to serve in Toronto, but after only one year in the city he returned to Louisiana to settle his affairs and bring his slaves to freedom in Canada.

King immediately set to work planning a settlement that would provide "land, education, and Christianity" for black refugees. The Presbyterian Church of Canada was supportive, and the Elgin Association was formed to buy the land. There was opposition, however, from the white population, led by local politician Edwin Larwill. They feared that the black settlement would devalue white owners' land values and endanger their children. A petition of protest was sent to Parliament but the settlement remained.

King arrived at Elgin on November 28, 1849 with the fifteen slaves he had brought north. The settlers built homes from logs cut from the thick bush surrounding the area. To support themselves, they produced potash and pearl ash from clearing the land and raised crops and livestock.

Others decided to settle at Elgin too, including Isaac Riley and his family. Riley was the first black man to purchase land and settle in the Elgin settlement, also in November 1849. He had been raised in Perry County, Missouri and

FUGITIVE SLAVES
IN
CANADA.

BUXTON MISSION.

A PUBLIC MEETING

WILL BE HELD IN THE

FREE CHURCH

GEORGE STREET, DUMFRIES,

On MONDAY Evening, September 3d,

At Eight o'Clock, when the

REV. WILLIAM KING

Formerly a Slave-owner in Louisiana, United States,

Will Address the Meeting on the subject of

Slavery in the United States, and the Social and Moral Improvement of the Fugitive Slaves in Canada.

At the close of the address a Collection will be taken up in aid of the Mission and Schools at Buxton, Canada West.

Dumfries, August 29, 1860.

Dumfries—Printed at the Standard Off , by Walter Easton.

Poster advertising a public meeting to discuss fugitive slaves in Canada held at the Buxton Mission, circa 1860.

escaped from a life of slavery to Canada with his wife and their child. Living among the French near Windsor, he was able to earn a small wage. He had then moved across the border to Michigan, where he found better pay. Eventually, Riley moved back to Canada—to St. Catharines, where he was paid fifty cents a day for his labour, then later to Buxton in order for his children to have a good education.

In 1850, King had opened the Buxton Mission School. It had both black and white students, and attracted excellent teachers from Knox Presbyterian College in Toronto. The school continued to grow and gained an excellent reputation. Adults who wanted to learn to read often attended evening classes. As the settlement flourished, its school offered such an excellent education that it attracted black and white students for miles around. In a few years, the school had sent several of its graduates on to university in Toronto.

That same year a post office and a church/school building were opened. In 1851, King was ordained and undertook fundraising tours in Canada, the United States, and Britain while helping Methodists and Baptists form congregations in the settlement. Two former slaves borrowed money from King to construct a brick factory, and by 1852 a sawmill, grist mill, and general store were in operation. By the next year, the settlement boasted 130 families. At its peak there were 300. By 1857, three schools were in operation.

The community was administered by shareholders

of the secular Elgin Association while the Buxton Mission, financed by the Presbyterian Church, handled religion and education. The settlement was known both as Elgin and as Buxton. According to the rules for the settlement, each settler was obliged to clear his land, build a house of at least four rooms, and help dig community drainage ditches; land could only be sold to blacks and had to remain in their hands for ten years; land had to be purchased, not leased; each house had to be at least 24 x 18 x 12 feet, with a porch across the front; and each house had to be built 33 feet from the road, with a picket fence and flower garden in front. Prizes were awarded for the most attractive home.

Many black settlers became citizens with voting rights, and in the provincial election of 1858 they were instrumental in defeating Edwin Larwill, who had opposed the black settlement, by voting for his opponent Archibald McKellar, who viewed them favourably.

But the community faced problems. Black journalists like Mary Ann Shadd were condemning all-black settlements and calling for integration with white society. Shadd felt that learning and acceptance would come as a result of integrated communities and feared that segregated settlements would remain that way. She focused not only on the Dawn Settlement of Josiah Henson and the Refugee Home Society of Henry Bibb, but also on William King's Elgin/Buxton settlement. She criticized these racially segregated communities in Canada West, opposed separate schools for blacks, and advocated full black integration into white society. She urged black Americans to reject the U.S. and look north to Canada. The *Provincial Freeman* was a forum for black readers' responses to articles and descriptions of their new lives.

Finally, in 1861, the fate of King's Elgin/Buxton settlement was sealed by the outbreak of the American Civil War. Seventy Elgin blacks enlisted in the Union Army and left immediately. The end of the war and emancipation then convinced many others to return to the southern United States. In 1873, the Elgin Association, having accomplished its goals and reimbursed its shareholders, disbanded. King continued his missionary work and was appointed pastor in Chatham, where he remained until his death in 1893.

The settlement still survives as a rural area with its original historic churches, a school, and some early homes. In spite of the initial resistance, the Elgin settlement was the most successful black settlement in Canada West. The site still exists today at North Buxton and is designated a National Historic Site.

Chapter 9
Black Settlers in Western Canada

On May 7, 1819, a young man of mixed race named James Douglas, not yet sixteen, sailed from Liverpool, England to apprentice with the North West Company, which was later absorbed into the Hudson's Bay Company (HBC). During his employment he explored by boat and horse, established forts, traded with the Native Americans (who threatened his life at one point), and crossed the Rocky Mountains seven times. He was soon promoted to company accountant in Vancouver. As he rose through the ranks, eventually holding the dual positions of Chief Factor and Governor of Vancouver Island, Douglas set high moral standards for the whites and

Aboriginals with whom he worked. Slavery upset him. He wrote to his bosses back in London, "With the Natives, I have hitherto endeavoured to discourage the practice by the exertion of moral influence alone. Against our own people I took a more active part, and denounced slavery as a state contrary to law." He once bought the freedom of a slave for fourteen shillings' worth of goods.

By 1858, almost forty years after starting his trading career, the "Scotch West Indian" was now Sir James Douglas—also known as "Black Douglas"—Governor of British Columbia, one of the most remote outposts of the British Empire. Through his efforts, Vancouver Island had become a colony with limited representation in Parliament, rather than the wilderness of trees and the single wooden fur-trading post it had been only a few years before. He had established large-scale farming, sawmills, coal mines, and salmon fishing. Compared with neighbouring Washington Territory where land was free, the colony's population was small, but it lived in peace with the Native Americans.

The discovery of gold changed everything. Some 8,000 miners had travelled the old brigade trail up the Okanagan Valley. American squatters had settled on San Juan Island, close to Victoria and the mouth of the Fraser River. The quaint village of Victoria exploded into a tent city filled with American merchants, land agents, and speculators. In the wild country across the Gulf of Georgia, the Aboriginal peoples were angered by the arrival of shiploads of Californian prospectors.

Douglas was concerned as well: "[If] the Country be thrown open to indiscriminate immigration, the interests of the empire may suffer," he warned London. He was equally concerned about HBC's private trading rights, and enlisted Captain James Charles Prevost of the British Boundary Commission to station a gunboat at the mouth of the Fraser River to check ship authorizations.

The mainland was still the territory of the Hudson's Bay Company and outside Douglas's authority, but he knew that many more American prospectors would follow. Both the colony of Vancouver Island and mainland British Columbia had few non-Aboriginal residents—there were only 500 Europeans living on the island and perhaps 150 on the mainland. They would soon be overwhelmed by gold-seekers who would bring their American laws—or lack of them—along.

What could Douglas do? He again wrote to London, warning: "If the majority of immigrants be American, there will always be a hankering in their minds after annexation to the United States. They will never cordially submit to English rule, nor possess the loyal feelings of British subjects." But London could not help him. He was on his own.

Fearing that his colony would be overwhelmed, he made a bold and inspired decision. He sent Captain Nagle of the wooden side-wheeler *Commodore* to San Francisco to invite 600 former black slaves to settle on Salt Spring Island and bolster the number of subjects loyal to Great Britain. This, thought Douglas, would thwart any threat, real or imagined, of a move by the United States to annex the isolated colony on the edge of the Pacific.

The San Franciscans responded immediately, sending thirty-five blacks as scouts to inspect the colony and report back. The delegates returned with glowing reports of strawberry vines and peach trees. Douglas was relieved when the *Commodore* returned with a group of black settlers, but his relief was tempered when he saw that 400 white prospectors were also on board.

Many more would follow. In 1862, the Cariboo gold rush attracted 5,000 miners. To accommodate this influx, Governor Douglas produced a plan for a major wagon road, 5.5 metres (18 feet) wide, to run 644 kilometres (400 miles) from Yale north to Quesnel and east to Williams Creek. This Great North Road, built by Royal Engineers and civilian contractors, would end any possibility of U.S. economic domination by making the Fraser River area British Columbia's commercial artery.

A man far ahead of his time, Douglas envisioned a link between British Columbia and Canada, saying, "Who can foresee what the next ten years may bring forth, an overland Telegraph, surely, and a Railroad on British Territory, probably, the whole way from the Gulf of Georgia to the Atlantic."

A British Columbian man looking for gold in a sluice box.

As Victoria confronted thousands of boisterous young miners with gold fever, Douglas reminded the newcomers that they were now in British territory. In June 1858, he created an all-black constabulary to police the town. Most of the policemen were African American and many returned to the U.S. following the American Civil War, but all were loyal to British laws giving black people their freedom. One black constable policed for several years on the Songhees Reserve, outside Victoria.

In the crucial early years of British Columbia's existence as a colony, the black settlers from San Francisco were for Douglas the "most orderly and useful and loyal section of the community" that he needed to keep the colony British. They were also encouraged by differences in the law on the two sides of the border. The United States Supreme Court had ruled that free, native-born black Americans could not be citizens, but in order to counterbalance the influx of white gold miners, British Columbia's colonial government under James Douglas, himself part black, was offering the black immigrants freedom, equality, and the right to vote.

Sir James Douglas remained governor of both Vancouver Island and British Columbia until his retirement in 1864 and is often referred to as "The Father of British Columbia." He died of a heart attack in 1877 and was buried at Ross Bay Cemetery in Victoria. Numerous places in the province are named in his honour—ports, mountain ranges, roads, and channels.

James Douglas was not the only mixed race or black employee to work for the fur-trading companies in the nineteenth century, however. There was also Pierre Bungo, for example, who worked for the Hudson's Bay Company in the

1840s. In the 1870s and 1880s more blacks entered the fur trade, including Dan Williams in the Peace River area; Henry Mills, who married into the Blood tribe; and William Bond, a whiskey trader in southern Alberta.

* * *

Many of the black immigrants from San Francisco were well-educated and prosperous, including merchant Mifflin Wistar Gibbs and his partner Peter Lester, who imported fine boots and shoes. Born in Philadelphia in 1823, Gibbs was raised at a local "station" of the Underground Railroad. His father, a preacher, died when Gibbs was a boy and his mother took in laundry to make ends meet. He educated himself in pre–Civil War America, becoming an abolitionist and a worker on the Underground Railway before moving to San Francisco.

In 1857, Gibbs and Lester had refused to pay the poll tax, since they were not allowed to vote. Their goods were seized and put up for auction but were saved when a southern white sympathizer persuaded the crowd not to bid. They set up business in their new homeland and prospered. Gibbs married one of the best-educated women in British Columbia, Maria Ann Alexander. He delighted in competing against the "old fogeys" of colonial Vancouver Island. In the spring of 1858, he used his carpentry skills to build his own store and made a fortune selling goods to the incoming prospectors.

Gibbs later built the first railway in the Queen Charlotte Islands, which only added to his now-considerable fortune. The general store also remained successful and he moved on to real estate, construction, and investment. For a time, he managed a coal mining operation in the Queen Charlotte Islands. Gibbs also bought a large quantity of land at Michigan and Menzies in the James Bay area, built a house on it, and hired one of the local Haida as his manservant.

During the American Civil War, Gibbs supported the African Rifles, British Columbia's first all-black militia unit. In the 1860s he stood for election in Victoria's municipal politics. On one occasion, while attending a fundraiser at a local theatre, white thugs threw flour over him and his pregnant wife and he fought them off with his fists. Despite the fracas, Gibbs became a councillor and acting mayor—and one of the first black politicians in Canada—and put Victoria's finances in order.

He then entered colonial politics, and was a member of the Yale Conference that framed the westernmost colony's entry into the Dominion of Canada. He had worked hard to turn a shanty town huddled around a fur-trading post into a capital city, but he still faced racial prejudice. It was a situation that eventually cost him his marriage. Mrs. Maria Alexander Gibbs was one of the most learned ladies in Victoria, yet whatever her husband's successes, no one ever invited her to tea. In fact, they were even ill-treated when

Maria was pregnant. Because of the uneasiness of their lives due to the colour of their skin, Maria finally returned to live in the U.S. Canada had been a refuge, but for her, it did not feel like home.

Canada had been a good port in a storm for Mifflin Wistar Gibbs, but it was not home for him either. Along with other black pioneers in British Columbia, his life had been soured by racism and segregation. With the end of the American Civil War in 1865, the appeal of Reconstruction America was strong. Gibbs and many of the pioneers returned south. He became America's first elected black judge, then United States consul in Madagascar. He died a rich man, aged ninety-four, in 1915.

Black families, like others, had the right to take up land under the British homesteading system. As long as they would clear, fence, and build on their land they could purchase it for low and deferred prices. But today, only a few descendants of the original black families—the Starks, the Harrisons, the Robinsons, and the Copelands—remain on Salt Spring Island.

* * *

The growth of ranching also brought blacks to the Canadian West. Of these settlers, John Ware is probably the best-known. Born a slave on a cotton plantation near Georgetown in South Carolina, Ware was freed at the end of the American Civil War. At the age of nineteen, uneducated but emancipated, he headed west to Texas seeking opportunity. In 1882, Ware drove 3,000 cattle north for the North West Cattle Company, later known as the Bar U Ranch.

Ware gained a reputation as a fine horseman and became known for his skills with a lasso, and tall tales followed him everywhere he went. He was said to have once stopped a cattle stampede with only a horse and six bullets. His admirers claimed that no horse had ever thrown him.

Experienced cowboys were in short supply on the Canadian range, so Ware was easily able to join the newly established Quorn Ranch which had a lease on 66,000 acres (26,709 hectares) southwest of present-day Calgary. It extended south from Sheep River to Tongue Creek and west from Cameron Coulee. The ranch was owned by a hunt club in England to raise cattle but mostly horses for sale on the English market. Ware was put in charge of the expensive imported breeding stock. Anticipating some of his wages to be paid in cattle, Ware had registered his own cattle brand, 9999 (known as Four-Nines or the Walking-Stick brand). After a 500-horse round-up from Fort Macleod to Calgary, a newspaper reported: "John is not only one of the best natured and most obliging fellows in the country, but he is one of the shrewdest cow men, and the man is considered pretty lucky who has him to look after his interest. The horse is not

John Ware and family, circa 1882.

running on the prairie which John cannot ride."

An early steer wrestler, he won his first competition in

1893 at the Calgary summer fair, the forerunner of the Calgary Stampede. Ware distinguished himself as a gentleman, and was well-regarded by other rural residents for his kindness and ranching skills. But because of his colour he still faced discrimination, especially in Calgary, where he was denied access to public areas, harassed by police, and arrested without cause. Not a man to be discouraged, Ware persevered and built a homestead on Sheep Creek near Turner Valley, south of Calgary, in the area that would in 1905 become the province of Alberta. He later relocated to an area along the Red Deer River near Duchess, east of Calgary, where there were fewer settlers. There, he lived with his wife Mildred Lewis, whom he had married in 1892, and their five children.

His life with Mildred ended in 1905 when she became ill and died of typhoid and pneumonia. Ware died later the same year while cutting a steer from a herd of cattle. His horse stumbled in a gopher hole and fell. John was crushed underneath the animal and died instantly. His funeral on September 14, 1905 at the Calgary Baptist Church was the largest funeral the city had ever seen. People from all over the province came to bid farewell to Alberta's legendary "Negro Cowboy," John Ware. He was honoured by having a mountain, a creek, and a coulee named for him. John Ware's cabin from his Brooks-area ranch was later moved to Dinosaur Provincial Park, where it has been preserved as an historic structure by the Alberta Parks Service.

Ware homestead near Brooks, Alberta.

* * *

Like Ware, the other first black settlers in Alberta were seen as curiosities rather than threats. They were few in number, but by 1910 their numbers had increased to the point where the Edmonton Board of Trade raised the first public complaint about the new settlers. It stated: "We want settlers that will assimilate with the Canadian people and in the negro we have a settler that will never do that." Politicians and immigration officials were reluctant to ban black immigration, because to do so would offend the United States government as well as black voters in Ontario and Nova Scotia. Instead, Canadian immigration agents often refused to grant Settler's

Certificates to black settlers, which entitled their bearers to discounted rail travel in Canada.

But in Edmonton, the Board of Trade continued its opposition to black settlement, supported by the Imperial Order of the Daughters of the Empire (IODE) and the municipal Trades and Labour Council. The Board prepared a petition to Prime Minister Sir Wilfrid Laurier, signed by 3,000 Edmontonians out of a total population of 25,000. It read, in part:

> *We urge upon your attention the serious menace to the future welfare of a large portion of western Canada, by reason of the alarming influx of Negro settlers...It is a matter of common knowledge that it has been proved in the United States that Negroes and whites cannot live in proximity without the occurrence of revolting lawlessness, and the development of bitter race hatred.*

The Canadian federal government took no action, but the aptly named William J. White, the senior Canadian official overseeing immigration in the U.S., suggested agents discourage black immigration at its source in Oklahoma. Agents were instructed to emphasize the hardships of northern life to "immigrants belonging to the Negro race, which race is deemed unsuitable to the climate and requirements of Canada."

Canadian railway companies asked American railways to discourage black emigration to Canada. In this, they had considerable success. African-American pastors as well as various government immigration and settlement ministers delivered the message that emigration to Canada meant trouble crossing the border, starvation and bitter cold, problems securing land, only one crop a year, and no release from discrimination if you got there. This propaganda only confirmed what many blacks in Oklahoma had been hearing from other sources.

In the end, the flow of black settlers from Oklahoma turned into a trickle. Only 1,000 to 1,500 blacks migrated to western Canada. In Alberta they settled in Amber Valley, and in Saskatchewan the largest black settlement consisted of twelve families known as the Shiloh People in Eldon, a site north of Maidstone.

Chapter 10
Black Settlers in the Maritimes

When the American colonies won their independence from British rule, many colonists no longer wanted to live in the new United States. Those who swore loyalty to the British Crown were offered land and provisions in Canada, and thousands took advantage of the British offer. These Loyalists left New England and headed north, but at the time the only established settlements were located on the eastern part of the remaining British colony. The pioneers arrived in Halifax by ship, bringing with them their belongings and everything they needed to start a new life while remaining under British rule. They brought with them about 3,000 indentured servants and black slaves, along with 300 free blacks. By 1784, some 3,500 blacks who had fought on the side of the British had moved to Maritime Canada after the war, most choosing to settle in Nova Scotia. The majority were former slaves, like the Fortune family, who had been given their freedom in return for military service fighting against their former owners. Rose Fortune was born a slave in Virginia, but after the American Revolution her parents had moved with other Black Loyalists to Nova Scotia. She was listed as the only child aged "over 10 years of parents Fortune and wife, Free Negroes," in the Annapolis Royal census of 1783. Many years later, as an adult, she reportedly helped escaped slaves who had arrived through Maine via the Underground Railroad to settle in Nova Scotia. By middle age, Rose, a single mother with two children, was running her own baggage-hauling business, the Cartage Company of Annapolis Royal.

She would meet the ships arriving from Boston and Saint John when they docked, pile carpet bags, trunks, boxes, and provisions into her wheelbarrow, and push them wherever their owners wanted to go—hotel or home, store or saloon. And she was all business. Any boys trying to cut into her territory for tips were routed immediately. Rose did not take any nonsense from anybody. An 1830 watercolour portrays her as a sturdy woman wearing men's low boots, a man's coat over her dress and apron, and a straw hat on top of a white lace cap with chin ties. She is carrying a straw basket and is looking ahead with determination.

Rose became the unofficial, self-appointed police-woman, who kept order around the port area and enforced curfews. Everybody knew Rose, accepted her voluntary law-enforcement role, and respected her—or soon learned to—and she was on friendly terms with prominent citizens. She expanded her cartage business to serve the whole town and added a wake-up service, so that travellers would not over-sleep and miss their ship.

In 1852, Lieutenant-Colonel Sleigh of the 77th Regiment wrote about his brief encounter with Rose:

> *I was aided in my hasty efforts to quit the*
> *abominable inn by a curious old Negro*
> *woman, rather stunted in growth...and*
> *dressed in a man's coat and felt hat; she had*
> *a small stick in her hand which she applied*
> *lustily to the backs of all who did not jump*
> *instantly out of the way. Poor old dame! She*
> *was evidently a privileged character.*

Rose died on February, 20, 1864, and was buried in an unmarked grave in Garrison Cemetery. Her age was unknown, but presumed to be about ninety. Her business carried on. Albert Lewis, who had married Rose's granddaughter, was a horseman who transformed the baggage-handling operation with horse-drawn wagons and coaches. Based at the railway station and the wharves, he now had the ability to pick up both passengers and freight. The business became known as Lewis Transfer in 1841, and was carried on by Rose Fortune's family for another century. After Albert Lewis's death in 1882, his son James took over, who was in turn succeeded by his son, James Jr. The black-owned company survived until 1960, and many of Rose Fortune's descendents still work in the shipping and trucking industry.

* * *

Many other black settlers, however, fared less well than Rose Fortune. The land grants that they received were generally small and on poor land with thin soil. In most cases, they got the land that nobody else wanted.

It had all begun with much optimism in 1783, when the town of Shelburne was founded by freed slaves and Black Loyalists. They had arrived in Shelburne Harbour full of ideals about human dignity, personal independence, and equal rights under the British crown. Governor Parr ordered the new arrivals to be settled "up the Northwest Harbour" in an area they named Birchtown, after Brigadier-General Samuel Birch. He had issued certificates to any black American who could prove minimum residence requirements and refugee status.

The General Birch Certificates were greatly prized.

A woodcutter at Shelburne, Nova Scotia, circa 1788.

Anyone holding one was guaranteed freedom and permission to go to Nova Scotia. From April to November 1783, the board overseeing embarkation heard claims from all those who hoped they qualified for the freedom offered. Officials also recorded the names and former owners of all freed slaves who were evacuated, so that their old masters could be compensated. Commander-in-Chief of the British forces, Sir Guy Carleton's "Book of Negroes" swelled with the names, ages, descriptions, and other pertinent details of 2,744 free black Americans who were included in the migration.

Meanwhile, Birch was issuing certificates of freedom to all blacks who qualified and could be evacuated to British ports in England, Florida, and Nova Scotia with the status of free men. Only fourteen cases were disputed, nine in favour of slave masters and two in favour of the ex-slave. The remaining three were rejected on the grounds that the Board had no authority.

On September 3, the Black Loyalists arrived in Birchtown and worked quickly to build shelter for themselves before the onset of winter. By the late fall of 1784, the town's population had grown to 1,521. For a short time it was the largest settlement of free blacks in North America, a fact that was noted in newspapers from New York to London. No exact plans of the settlement still exist today, but the town may have covered an area as small as 13 acres (5.3 hectares) or as large as 400 acres (162 hectares).

The Black Loyalists were led by Colonel Stephen Blucke, a free man of mixed race from Barbados who had been an officer in the Black Pioneers, who was described as "a man of upright character, intelligent, and of good education." He served dual roles, first as colonel of the Black Militia in Shelburne (Port Roseway), and second as school teacher in Birchtown from 1785 to 1792, when poor attendance forced the school's closure.

Blucke was instrumental in getting people the lots they were promised. Most of the settlers were allocated 40 acres, but his own allotment was 200 acres. He helped many people draw up petitions to the authorities for supplies and aid, and some documents refer to him as the Birch Magistrate, implying that he dispensed rudimentary justice in the settlement and that he was often a witness to land deals. Blucke was the only member of Birchtown who could attend the Anglican Church in Shelburne because only he had enough money to rent a pew there. In 1792, however, Stephen Blucke was accused of stealing money that had been entrusted to him and decided to leave the settlement. One night he disappeared. Later, some pieces of his clothing were discovered near the Annapolis Road. There were suspicions that he may have been killed by wild animals or murdered. But by whom? The money he was accused of stealing was later found, but his body never was.

The Birchtown settlers were a diverse group. Among their number was David George, who was to become the founder of the first Black Baptist Church of Canada. George had been born into a family of slaves, but he ran away from his master at the age of nineteen. In 1773, he had been one of the founders of the Silver Bluff Baptist Church in South Carolina, the first black church in North America. After the American Revolution, in the spring of 1783, he came to Shelburne and began preaching, quickly gaining fame around the province. However, he was soon forced to flee for his life. He was beaten during riots that had broken out in Shelburne when disbanded white soldiers decided that blacks were undercutting their wages. A report at the time stated: "An Extraordinary mobb or Riot has happened in Shelburne. Some thousands of People Assembled with Clubs and drove the Negroes out of the Town..." George sought refuge in Birchtown, but his outspokenness annoyed the residents and four months later they drove him back to Shelburne.

The dreams of the Black Loyalists were quickly dashed by a combination of circumstances. There was the bitterly cold winter weather to endure. And there were delays in granting farm lots, which did not officially take place until 1787. What's more, these lots were located eight kilometres (five miles) from Birchtown, where the land is covered by countless granite boulders and very thin topsoil—far from ideal farming country. And many of the Black Loyalists were labourers and harbour pilots, skills they could only put to use in Shelburne, so they had to make the long trek to town and back again every day to work.

To make matters worse, the riot by ex-soldiers in 1784, protesting competition for jobs from the residents of Birchtown, made even this way of earning a living impossible. When crown rations were no longer made available to the people of the town in response, Birchtown began to decline. The inevitable result for its Black Loyalist inhabitants was famine. Boston King, a Birchtown settler who was a carpenter, ship builder, and occasional fisherman observed that "...some killed and ate their dogs and cats; poverty and distress prevailed on every side."

Birchtown was not the only black settlement in Nova

Scotia to find itself in dire straits. Others were suffering the same fate, and all began searching for a new promised land which, in 1791, seemed to be the newly created Republic of Sierra Leone in Africa, the continent from which their ancestors had originally been taken. John Clarkson, a representative for the Sierra Leone Company, met with the people of Birchtown in their meeting house, where he outlined the alternatives offered to them by the British Government:

1. Accept the land they had been promised in Nova Scotia;
2. Enlist in the British Army in the West Indies; or
3. Accept the offer of land in, and free transportation to, Sierra Leone.

Clarkson described the decision made by the Birchtown residents: "...they were unanimous in the desire for embarking for Africa, telling me their labour was lost upon the land in this country and their utmost efforts would barely keep them in existence—being now sunk to the lowest wretchedness they had made up their minds for quitting this country." In fact, the response across the province was overwhelming. In total, 1190 people signed up to sail to Sierra Leone, 544 of them from Shelburne and Birchtown. This represented half of the area's black population.

The departure of fifteen ships from Halifax in 1792

signalled the end of Birchtown. Among the emigrants was the preacher David George. Another settler who left was Boston King. In Birchtown, King had been so emotionally affected by the preaching of Freeborn Garretson, a powerful American preacher, that he began voluntary missionary work in the province. In 1791, he had been appointed pastor in charge of the Methodist Society at Preston. But King, his family, and his congregation all emigrated to Sierra Leone.

The exodus to Sierra Leone was later joined by another black community, the Jamaican Maroons. This group consisted of almost 600 runaway slaves who had fought the British and were then deported to Nova Scotia. On June 26, 1796, the *Dover*, *Mary*, and *Anne* sailed from Port Royal Harbour in Jamaica to Halifax, where 5,000 acres (20 sq. km) had been set aside for the community of Preston. But farming was not the Maroons' way of life, so they were instead employed in building the new fortifications of the Halifax Citadel. After four years, the Maroons moved to Freetown, the capital of Sierra Leone.

Other black refugees who had come to the Canadian Maritimes, however, remained. A group of former American slaves who had joined the British side, known as the Black Refugees, arrived after the War of 1812. Some 1,500 of them resettled in Nova Scotia and another 500 in New Brunswick. These groups formed early black communities.

In all, some 130 Underground Railroad stations in

Maine led runaways to Canada's Maritime Provinces. The refugees settled primarily near Halifax, along the Saint John River, and in Fredericton.

One of the best-known of these communities was founded in the 1830s, when a number of descendants of American slaves settled on the northern edge of Halifax, on the shores of the Bedford Basin. Land was cheap there, and had originally been designated for whites but was not yet occupied. It was close to city employment, and the settlers formed the community that became known as Africville.

According to city records, William Brown and William Arnold, descendants of black refugees from the War of 1812, bought the first two lots that led to the establishment of the community. Initially known as the Campbell Road settlement, it quickly acquired its new name because of its black population and "Africville" was incorporated into municipal records.

Africville was a self-contained black village within city limits, but the city provided it with no services: no water, no sewage, no paved roads, no snow removal, no police. Africville developed slowly after the War of 1812, and in 1848 the first legal deeds for the community were issued.

In 1849, preacher Richard Preston established a Baptist church in Africville which eventually became the Seaview African United Baptist Church. In the 1850s, some Africville residents were relocated to make way for railway construction. By 1851 the census listed eight families in Africville, but by

Partial view of Africville settlement, Halifax, Nova Scotia, 1964.

the 1870s, in addition to the church, there were new homes, a school, and two stores. The community grew further after the American Civil War.

Africville thrived from the 1890s to the 1920s. At its peak, just before the First World War, 300 people in eighty families resided in Africville. Because of the war industry, jobs were available but the residents also took pride in their homes, gardens, their church, and the good fishing in the basin. Africville survived the Halifax Explosion of 1917 in the harbour's Narrows—the biggest manmade explosion in history until the nuclear bomb in Hiroshima in 1945—protected by a bluff of land. The community suffered badly during the Depression, but rebounded from the late 1930s until after the

Second World War, when they began a slow downturn that lasted through the 1950s and into the late 1960s.

Throughout Africville's history the city of Halifax saw fit to locate a number of unappealing sites around and within the community—sites that other (white) Halifax residents did not want in their neighbourhoods. Over the years, Africville became home to Rockhead Prison (1853), the city's soil disposal pits (1858), an infectious disease hospital (1870s), a trachoma hospital (1905), an open city dump and incinerator (early 1950s), and a slaughterhouse.

Now, the physical presence of Africville is no more. In 1964, the city of Halifax relocated the residents of this tight-knit community of law-abiding, tax-paying Baptists and destroyed their dwellings, which were labelled slums. In 1968, Seaview Church was demolished in the middle of the night by city workers. The last house was bulldozed on January 2, 1970. What was seen as a slum by outsiders was a place of privacy to those who lived there, free from racism and discrimination. The forefathers of the people of Africville had been promised equality but lived on the outskirts of society—both literally and figuratively.

Finally, in February 2010, the people of Africville and their descendants received a formal apology from the mayor of Halifax Regional Municipality for the injustice they had suffered when they were uprooted from their homes and their community was destroyed.

Epilogue

When people like the fictional character Susa, and other former slaves like her, finally escaped from bondage in Canada, they were filled with hope for their future and that of their children and grandchildren. How could they foresee that in the centuries to come there would still be problems?

Whether they arrived as former slaves or as free citizens, prejudice against blacks was common, and racism was unrelenting. The real story of Viola Desmond, a Canadian who stood up against discrimination, is perhaps the best known. But the true significance of her act of defiance and her subsequent arrest is only now starting to be widely recognized. Nine years before Rosa Parks made her legendary protest against racism by sitting in the "whites only" section of a bus in Montgomery, Alabama, Viola Desmond made an equally definitive stand against racial segregation in New Glasgow, Nova Scotia.

The Underground Railroad

Viola Desmond was born in 1914 and grew up in a prosperous Halifax family. She wanted to be a hairdresser, one of the few professions open to an ambitious, independent black woman. Unable to gain admission to a hairdressing school in Nova Scotia, she trained in Montreal, New York, and Atlantic City. Viola then returned to Halifax, married, and opened her first salon, specializing in hairstyles and hair treatments for blacks. After a few successful years, she founded a school to train beauticians. Her vision was a chain of salons across Canada staffed by her graduates, all specialists in styling black women's hair.

But on November 8, 1946, Viola Desmond made history. The successful thirty-two-year-old Halifax businesswoman's car broke down in New Glasgow, Nova Scotia. While her vehicle was being repaired, she decided to go see a movie at the Roseland Theatre. Desmond requested a ticket for the main floor of the theatre, paid for it, went in, and sat down. Although it was not posted, the theatre had a policy that people of colour were only allowed to sit in the balcony. When ordered to move, Desmond said she could not see from the balcony, she had paid to sit on the main floor, and there she would stay.

The manager called a policeman, and together the two men carried Viola Desmond out onto the street, injuring her knee and hip in the process. She was arrested and spent the night in the town jail. She was not informed of her rights, or at least any remaining to her. She was not allowed to post bail. She was confined in the same jail block as male prisoners. Determined to maintain her dignity, she sat up straight for the entire night, all the while wearing her elegant white gloves.

In the morning she was brought before a magistrate. She had no legal representation and no knowledge that she could question the complainants. She was found guilty, but guilty of what?

She was not convicted of sitting in the "whites only" main floor section of the theatre. The crime for which Viola Desmond was convicted was tax evasion—she had not paid the one-cent tax for a ticket to sit on the main floor, she had paid for a less expensive seat in the balcony. It made no difference that she had requested a seat on the main floor, believed she had paid for a ticket on the main floor, did not know and was not told that blacks were restricted to the balcony, had offered to pay the difference in ticket price, and had then been injured and held unjustly. The magistrate sentenced Viola Desmond to thirty days in jail or a fine of $20, plus $6 to the manager of the theatre. Viola elected to pay the fine.

The doctor who treated her physical injuries recommended that she consult a lawyer. At the urging of friends, Desmond challenged the verdict in the Supreme Court of Nova Scotia. Although one of the four judges, Justice Hall, referred to the issue of race, he agreed with his three colleagues that there had been no error in law at the original trial. The court unanimously upheld the verdict. Her conviction stood.

The unspoken truth was that Viola Desmond was found guilty of being a black person who had stepped out of her assigned place in Canadian society. The Supreme Court defeat left her discouraged. Her marriage, already strained by her success in business, ended because her husband thought she was making too much of a small matter. But her supporters did not give up. Friend and newspaper publisher Carrie Best, activist Pearleen Oliver, and the Nova Scotia Association for the Advancement of Coloured People (NSAACP) campaigned to raise money for an appeal. Her white Halifax lawyer, Frederick Bissett, donated his fees back to the NSAACP.

With this money, Viola continued the fight she had started, and further action eventually led to the repeal of segregation policies in Nova Scotia in 1954, more than a year before Rosa Parks helped coalesce the civil rights movement in the United States.

After the trial, Viola Desmond relinquished her business and her dream of a national chain of salons. She enrolled in a Montreal business school, then moved to New York City, where she established a talent agency for performers. In 1965, shortly after arriving, she died. She was fifty years old. Viola Desmond has been immortalized in the work of poet and playwright David Woods, who was inspired by her story. His poem "Witness" is a tribute to her life and spirit.

Epilogue

In April 2010, forty-five years after her death, the Province of Nova Scotia apologized to Viola Desmond for her shameful and unjust conviction and granted her a free pardon.

North America Slavery Timeline

1501 Spanish settlers bring slaves from Africa to Santo Domingo (now the Dominican Republic/Dominica) in the New World.

1608 French settlers bring their black family slaves with them to New France (now Canada).

1619 Africans brought to Jamestown, Virginia, were the first slaves imported into Britain's North American colonies.

1628 Olivier Le Jeune is the first slave transported directly from Africa to New France.

1700 A Massachusetts jurist, Samuel Seawell, prints the first North American anti-slavery publication, *The Selling of Joseph.*

1705 Virginia lawmakers identify slaves as property, thus allowing owners to bequeath their slaves along with other real estate, and allowing masters to "kill and destroy" runaway slaves. Slavery is legalized in New France by the *Code Noir*.

1734 Marie-Joseph Angélique, slave of a wealthy Montreal merchant, sets fire to her owner's house after learning she is to be sold. The fire destroys most of the central city. She is hanged.

1775 Anthony Benezet of Philadelphia founds the first abolitionist society and Benjamin Franklin heads the organization in 1787.

1776 The Declaration of Independence by the Continental Congress asserts "that these United Colonies are, and of Right ought to be, Free and Independent States" separate from England, and maintains the right to own slaves.

1783 The Black Pioneers, an all-black regiment loyal to England during the U.S. War of Independence, are given land in the British colony of Nova Scotia.

1792 The British government offers free passage to blacks to relocate in Sierra Leone and fifteen ships leave Halifax; sixty-five passengers die en route.

1793 The U.S. government issues the Fugitive Slave Act outlawing all efforts to interfere with the recapture of runaway slaves. The Act is strengthened in 1850.

1793 In Upper Canada (now Ontario) Lt-Gov. John Graves Simcoe enacts The Law Against Slavery legislation making it illegal to bring persons into the colony to be enslaved. Existing slaves are not freed, however. The Act remains in effect until 1833 when the British Empire abolishes slavery.

1800–65 More than 30,000 blacks come to Canada on the Underground Railroad.

1803 Lower Canada (Quebec) abolishes slavery.

1808 The importation of African slaves (the Slave Trade) is outlawed by the U.S. but smuggling of human property continues.

1812 Company of "Colored Troops" formed in Upper Canada under white commander Captain Robert Runchey to fight for Canada and the British in the War of 1812–15, and to prevent returning to slavery.

1820 By the Missouri Compromise, the state of Missouri

is admitted to the U.S. as a slave state and Maine as a free state. Slavery is against the law in any subsequent territories north of latitude 36°30'.

1830 Josiah Henson, considered the inspiration for Harriet Beecher Stowe's book *Uncle Tom's Cabin*, makes it to Canada from Kentucky.

1833–34 Through the British Imperial Act, England abolishes slavery throughout the British Empire including its colonies in Jamaica, Barbados, and other West Indian territories, as well as in Canada.

1837 Black volunteers serve in the "Colored Corps" during the Rebellion to defend the existing government and support black rights.

1841 The British-American Institute, where blacks could live and learn, is established by Josiah Henson at the Dawn Settlement.

1848 The first legal deeds for the black community of Africville near Halifax, Nova Scotia are issued. William Brown Sr. purchases the first property.

1849 *The Life of Josiah Henson, Formerly a Slave,*

Henson's autobiography, is published.

1850 Through the Compromise of 1850, in exchange for California joining the US.. as a free state, a revised Fugitive Slave Act—harsher than the 1793 version—is enacted. Canada becomes a haven for American slaves.

1851-53 Henry Bibb escapes to Detroit then Windsor, and founds *Voice of the Fugitive*. In the same year, the Anti-Slavery Society of Canada is formed by abolitionist sympathizers to "aid in the extinction of slavery all over the world." Great Lakes steamers begin transporting blacks into Canada from the U.S. Mary Ann Shadd and her brother Isaac found the abolitionist newspaper the *Provincial Freeman* in Windsor, making her the first black female publisher in North America.

1854 Through the Kansas-Nebraska Act, Congress sets aside the Missouri Compromise of 1820 and allows the two new territories to choose whether to permit or reject slavery. Violent protests erupt.

1857 The Dred Scott Decision by the U.S. Supreme Court decides (seven to two) that blacks can never be citizens and that Congress has no authority to outlaw slavery in any territory.

1858 In a move to increase the population loyal to Britain and stave off possible annexation of the isolated British colony by the U.S., British Columbia black colonial governor James Douglas invites 600 freed slaves living in San Francisco to move north and settle on Salt Spring Island near Victoria.

1860s Black businessman Mifflin Gibbs, who had moved from San Francisco to Victoria, enters municipal politics and becomes Canada's first black politician.

1860 Abraham Lincoln of Illinois is elected president, becoming the first Republican Party representative to hold that office.

1861–65 U.S. Civil War between the Union north and the Confederate south lasts four years and claims 623,000 lives.

1862 President Lincoln drafts the preliminary Emancipation Proclamation on September 22nd. The final Proclamation, issued on January 1, 1863, effectively frees all slaves.

1863 The Emancipation Proclamation frees slaves in Confederate-controlled (Rebel) states fighting against the Union north. It does not free any slaves in states that remained in the Union.

1865 Slavery is abolished by the 13th Amendment to the United States Constitution.

1882 Black cowboy John Ware introduces longhorn cattle to Canada and starts the first rodeo in Calgary.

1890 The Brussels Act gives anti-slavery countries the right to stop and search ships for slaves.

1905–11 Disaffected blacks from Oklahoma undertake the "Black Trek" to the Canadian prairies in search of land, where they meet the same discrimination they had faced in the U.S.

1913 Harriet Tubman, a "conductor" with the Underground Railroad who made nineteen surreptitious trips to the American south to guide some 300 slaves into Canada, dies in New York.

1925 The Slavery Convention binds all signatories to end slavery and suppress the slave trade.

1946 Viola Desmond, a black business woman from

Halifax, is arrested in New Glasgow, Nova Scotia, for sitting in the white only section of the movie theatre.

1948 Article 4 of the United Nations Declaration of Human Rights bans slavery globally.

1964 The Nova Scotia borough of Africville, called a slum by the city of Halifax, is destroyed, its residents relocated, and the land amalgamated into the growing municipality.

Bibliography

Backhouse, Constance. *Colour-Coded: A Legal History of Racism in Canada, 1900-1950.* University of Toronto Press: Toronto, 2007.

Blight, David W. *Passages to Freedom: The Underground Railroad in History and Memory.* HarperCollins Canada: Toronto, 2006.

Bode, Patrick. "Simcoe and the Slaves." *The Beaver* 73.3 (June-July 1993).

Buckmaster, Henrietta. *Let My People Go.* Beacon Press: Boston, 1969.

Chadwick, Bruce. *Traveling the Underground Railroad: A Visitor's Guide to More Than 300 Sites.* Citadel Press: New York, 1999.

Cooper, Aufa. *Hanging of Angélique: The Untold Story of Canadian Slavery and the Burning of Old Montreal.* HarperCollins Canada: Toronto, 2006.

_____. *My Name Is Henry Bibb: A Story of Slavery and Freedom.* Kids Can Press: Toronto, 2009.

_____-. *My Name Is Sarah Wheatley: A Story of Slavery and Freedom.* Kids Can Press: Toronto, 2009.

Curtis, Anna L. *Stories of the Underground Railroad.* Kessinger Publishing: Montana, 2007.

Bibliography

Derrek, Tom. "In Bondage." *The Beaver* 83.1 (February-March 2003).

Drew, Benjamin. *A North-Side View of Slavery. The Refugee: Narratives of Fugitive Slaves in Canada.* Dundurn Press: Toronto, 2008.

"From Slavery to Freedom." *Heritage Matters,* Special Edition. Ontario Heritage Trust: August 2007.

Hendrick, George. *Fleeing for Freedom: Stories of the Underground Railroad As Told by Levi Coffin and William Still.* Ivan R. Dee Publisher: Chicago, 2003.

Henson, Josiah. *The Life of Josiah Henson: Formerly a Slave, Now an Inhabitant of Canada (1849).* Kessinger Publishing: Montana, 2007.

Hepburn, Sharon A. Roger. *Crossing the Border: A Free Black Community in Canada.* University of Illinois Press: Champlaign, IL, 2007.

Hudson, J. Blaine. *Fugitive Slaves and the Underground Railroad in the Kentucky Borderland.* McFarland & Company: Jefferson, NC, 2002.

Iacovetta, Franca. *A Nation of Immigrants: Readings in Canadian History, 1840s-1960s.* University of Toronto Press: Toronto, 1998.

Lowry, Beverly. *Harriet Tubman, Imaging a Life.* Anchor Press: Norwell, MA, 2008.

Shadd, Adrienne, Afua Cooper, and Karolyn Smardz Frost. *The Underground Railroad: Next Stop Toronto!.*

Natural Heritage Books: Toronto, 2002.

Smardz Frost, Karolyn, et al, Ed. *Ontario's African-Canadian Heritage, Collected Writings by Fred Landon, 1918-1967*. Natural Heritage Books: Toronto, 2009.

Smardz Frost, Karolyn. *I've Got A Home In Glory Land: A Lost Tale of the Underground Railroad*. Farrar, Straus and Giroux: New York, 2007.

Still, William. *Underground Railroad, 1872*. Echo Library: London, 2007.

Stowe, Harriet Beecher. *Uncle Tom's Cabin*. Dover Publications: New York, 2005.

Tobin, Jacqueline L. and Raymond G. Dobard. *Hidden in Plain View: A Secret Story of Quilts and the Underground Railroad*. Anchor Press: Norwell, MA, 2000.

Tobin, Jacqueline L. *From Midnight to Dawn: The Last Tracks of the Underground Railroad*. Anchor Books: New York, 2007.

Winks, Robin W. *The Blacks in Canada: A History*. McGill-Queens University Press: Montreal, 1997.

Acknowledgements

I would like to thank Rosemary Sadlier for her helpful comments about this manuscript. I would also like to thank the research services available at the Library and Archives Canada in Ottawa for their endless patience and depth of knowledge on a diverse list of subjects. I also appreciate access to the personal library of Robert C. Mercier (Bob, to me) and its convenient borrowing terms.

About the Author

L. D. Cross is an Ottawa writer and member of the Professional Writers Association of Canada (PWAC) and the Canadian Authors Association (CAA). Her business and lifestyle articles have appeared in publications such as *Home Business Report, Profit, Modern Woman, WeddingBells, Fifty-Five Plus, enRoute, AmericanStyle, Aviation History, The Hill Times,* and *Legion Magazine.*

She has won awards of excellence for features and for editorial and technical writing in the International Association of Business Communicators (IABC) Ottawa EXCEL competitions and for articles about seniors in the U.S. National Mature Media Awards.

She has written three other titles in the Amazing Stories series: *Ottawa Titans: Fortune and fame in the early days of Canada's capital; Spies in Our Midst: The incredible story of Igor Gouzenko, Cold War spy;* and *The Quest for the Northwest Passage: Exploring the elusive route through Canada's Arctic waters.*

Cross is also co-author of *Inside Outside: In conversation with a Doctor and a Clothing Designer* and *Marriage is a Business!*

Illustration Credits

Index

Index